THE IRISH FAMINE

AN ILLUSTRATED

HISTORY

THE IRISH FAMINE

AN ILLUSTRATED

HISTORY

Helen Litton

WOLFHOUND PRESS

IRISH BOOKS AND MEDIA

941
L781
1994

First published 1994 by
WOLFHOUND PRESS Ltd
68 Mountjoy Square
Dublin 1

© Helen Litton 1994

British Library Cataloguing-in-Publication Data
    Litton, Helen
    Brief History of the Great Irish Famine
    I. Title
    363.809415

ISBN 0 86327 427 7

Published in the USA 1994 by
IRISH BOOKS AND MEDIA, Inc.
1433 Franklin Avenue East
Minneapolis, Minnesota 55404-2135

ISBN 0 937702 14 5

Library of Congress Catalog card number: 94-76754

Credits
The author and publishers gratefully acknowledge the assistance of Bord Fáilte and *Ireland of Welcomes*, AFrI Great 'Famine' Project, Gilbert Library, The Society of Friends, RV Comerford, John Gough, Naomi O'Donovan. For illustration credits, see page 139

The publishers have made every reasonable effort to contact the copyright holders of material reproduced in this book. If any involuntary infringement of copyright has occurred, sincere apologies are offered and the owners of such copyright are requested to contact the publishers.

Cover design: Daire Ní Bhéartúin
Typesetting: Wolfhound Press
Printed in the Republic of Ireland by Colour Books, Dublin

CONTENTS

INTRODUCTION

The Great Famine which devastated Ireland between the years 1845 and 1850 is one of the most tragic events in Irish history, the one every Irish schoolchild remembers, the source of numberless stories, songs and poems, and an ever-present stick with which to beat the English. Why was the loss of potato crops such an important event? Why was there nothing else to eat? How could such remorseless destruction of a people and their society occur? Did nobody try to stop it?

This book sets out to describe, straightforwardly, how the potato blight affected the livelihood of thousands of people, how their lives were so insecure, how large sums of money and the intense efforts of hundreds of well-meaning people failed to prevent huge loss of life.

By 1850, when the worst of the Famine had ended, Ireland had lost more than two million of her people, out of a total of eight million. Perhaps a million and a half had died from fever and starvation and cold, but the full numbers will never be known. At least another million had fled to other countries, despairing of any future in their homeland.

Hundreds of landlords were bankrupt, and the insecure land system was a shambles.

The Famine and its aftermath laid bare the huge gulf that lay between Ireland, largely inhabited by a poverty-stricken population living constantly on the edge, with no rights of land ownership, and the United Kingdom of which it was supposed to be a part. Britain's rapidly changing society, with its growing industrial might and its developing cities, was irritated by what it saw as the whining, begging, shiftless Irish, who would rise in rebellion as soon as look at you. The roots of prejudice ran deep, on both sides, and the convictions of each side were largely confirmed by the great tragedy which began to unfold in 1845.

Deaths	
1843	70,499
1844	75,055
1845	86,900
1846	122,899
1847	249,335
1848	208,252
1849	240,797
1850	164,093
1851 (to 30 March) .	46,261
1851 (31 Mar-31 Dec)	50,537
1852	80,112

Source: Census of Ireland 1841-71. These figures tend to under-estimate deaths, since it was not compulsory to record births or deaths before 1864. No record appeared for an entire family who had emigrated or died since the previous census.

Population of Ireland 1841-1871	
1841	8,175,000
1851	6,552,000
1861	5,799,000
1871	4,412,000

CHAPTER 1

1845

Background to Famine

If you could be brought back to Ireland in 1844, you would find a country with a large, vigorous population, and land which ranged from fertile farms in the north and east to large tracts of bog and rock in the west and south. The native culture was rich in history and tradition, and the Irish language was still widely spoken. Catholic emancipation had been granted in 1829, and the Catholic faith was practised by 80% of the population. However, the bulk of that population lived in conditions of poverty and insecurity.

At the top of the social pyramid was the Ascendancy class, the English and Anglo-Irish families who owned most of the land, and had almost limitless power over their tenants. Some of their estates were huge — the Earl of Lucan, for example, owned over 60,000 acres. Many of these landlords lived in England and were called 'absentees'. They used agents to administer their property, and most of them had no interest in it except to spend the money the rents brought in.

It was a very unbalanced social structure, with a huge gap between the landowners and the next level, the farmers. The farmers rented the land they worked, and those who could afford to rent large farms would break up some of the land into smaller plots. These were then leased to 'cottiers' or small farmers, under a system called 'conacre'.

Nobody had security of tenure, and rents were high. In the north, the 'Ulster Custom' gave tenant farmers the right to sell the goodwill of their land, if they had to leave, but this did not fully protect them against eviction. In the heavily-populated south and west, farms were scratched out of boggy or stony land. Very little cash money was used in the economy. The cottier paid his rent by working for his landlord, and he could also rear a pig to sell for the small amount of cash he might need to buy clothes or other necessary goods. Cottiers from the poorer parts of Ireland would go to England each summer, to labour on farms there.

There was also a large population of agricultural labourers, who travelled around looking for work. These were very badly off, because not many Irish farmers could afford labour, and they would try to get the smallest patch of land to keep their families together. In 1835, an inquiry found that over two million people were without regular employment of any kind.

There was no social welfare system, of course, and if a family became completely destitute, the only place for them was the workhouse. Education was very limited, and only about 28% per cent of the population could read and write.

No-one owned the land they worked on, and tenants could be put out at any time for such reasons as non-payment of rent, or because the landlord had decided to raise sheep on the estate. There was no incentive to improve land, and instead a system of subdivision grew up.

Such a scene of misery as this day unfolded, or rather such a series of miserable scenes. Annie and I went to hunt out children for the infant class and every where almost we found people struggling for existence, some a little better off than others in consequence of better management, but badly at best and no seeming hope anywhere of better days, no prospect for the children beyond toil, toil for the bit to eat. But all the wretchedness we found during our walk in the morning was nothing compared to the scene at Harry Kiogh's dwelling where I went after dinner to see his poor wife Betty, who is near dying after a miscarriage caused by overweighting herself with the turf she brought home on her back through the river, their fuel for the winter. It is an old cow-house, part of a ruined building quite apart from all neighbourhood, has never been dashed inside or out, no window, no chimney, a sort of door that don't fit and some thatch by way of — the husband has built a rough stone wall elbow high to protect the bed from the wind of the door. I saw no bedclothes, straw below, a sort of old dark cloth above; there was a pot and a plate or two and a basin and a spoon and the remains of an old dresser, four starved looking children, very clean, the poor fainting woman hardly able to speak and not able to raise herself. She did speak and it was to give thanks! for returning strength and a job of work her husband had got which would bring him 30/- pay, the rent 20/-!! for that place!! and leave a trifle to thatch over the bed! and she had the fowl still and her four ducks and her pig that Tom Kiogh gave them last year, plenty of turf which she would soon be able to bring home and a fine crop of potatoes when they could release them, and please God harvest work would help them to do that if she were but once able to leave her bed. All this I saw, but there are a hundred cases, aye more than a hundred worse which I have not seen. Is there no remedy for such utter wretchedness? Education alone won't do, the body must be fed at any rate before the mind can act.

Mrs Smith was the wife of a landowner in County Wicklow, one of the more prosperous areas of Ireland.

Cottiers and farmers who had no money for marriage dowries, or for educating children to other careers, would simply give them a portion of land when they got married. Since you could never have security, or a guaranteed permanent home, there was no need to delay marriage. People married young, and constructed primitive huts on whatever patch of land they could find. As Irish peasant families were normally large, this meant the portions of land got ever smaller, and land became poorer as it was over-worked. The marginal cost of having children was lower than in the rest of Europe, because of the cheap food and fuel available, and the low standards of housing and clothing. Children were a guarantee of support in old age. But infant mortality was high, about 200 deaths in every 1,000 births.

Housing was very poor, either thatched cottages or small one-roomed huts made of stone and turf, and roofed with branches and more turf. These huts had no windows, just a hole in the roof for the smoke of the cooking fire to escape. Fortunately the climate was mild, and turf for fires was easily collected from the bogs that covered the country. In fact, visitors to Ireland at that time commented on the cheerfulness and health of the rural population. Hospitality to the passing stranger was always generous, however little there was to offer.

While the bulk of the population lived rural lives, Ireland did have towns, the largest being Belfast, Dublin and Cork. Industry was beginning to develop — Belfast had its linen industry — and a middle class was developing as well. However, only about one-eighth of the population lived in urban areas. In the poorest parts of rural Ireland, there could be up to 700 people per square mile. The road system was very good, with thirty coach routes to the main towns, but there were at this stage only seventy miles of railway track, while Britain already had 2,000 miles. Many remote areas were almost completely inaccessible.

Donnybrook Fair, by Benjamin Clayton, 1833

The Devon Commission, which examined the Irish economic system in 1843, concentrated on the land system and the landlords as the chief cause of the widespread poverty and lack of security. However, its recommendations for change were overtaken by the Great Famine which racked Ireland between 1845 and 1850. By the end of this catastrophe, over one million people had died, and another million or more had emigrated. The land system had been greatly shaken; large numbers of landlords had gone bankrupt, and the agricultural labourer class had been almost wiped out. Small farms were being consolidated into larger ones, and the Irish language had begun to disappear.

From March till May ... he generally earns from £1.10 shillings to £2; of this £1 goes to pay the rent of his cabin, and for as much as can be spared of the remainder he buys wool, tow and flax which, in the course of the summer his wife manufactures into frieze, drugget and coarse linen to clothe the family; but every year does not afford this. A good part of May and June is taken up with setting and landing his potatoes and cutting his turf; this turf the wife and children rear during the succeeding months. By the latter end of May his stock of potatoes is out, and he then gets more, or some oatmeal, on credit at high interest; he then repairs to the counties of Meath and Dublin, or perhaps to England, for haymaking and harvesting and returns in the month of September ... in time to avoid a civil-bill process by paying up the price of the oatmeal he was credited for; from this, until the potatoes are dug, he may earn from £1 to £1. 10 shillings, and his pig, now a year old, sells for about £3, making, in all, about £4. 10 shillings or £5. But now his half-yearly rent is again become due, above £1, his conacre rent more than £2; his frieze and linen are ready, and the tailor and weaver must be paid. He wants a pair of brogues for the winter, the wife an apron, shawl or cap, but, as to shoes, it is a small chance for her; he himself wants a fine shirt for Sunday. The earnings of his elder children at service are too small to clothe them; and the wife (let things go as they will) must get 5 shillings to buy flax, that, with spinning it through the winter, and selling an odd hank and a few eggs, she may struggle from week to week to get salt, soap, blue, starch, an odd herring, and, with great saving and care, a few pounds of meat at Christmas. Besides this, he has to replace the pig, or how is he to pay for his conacre next year?

A bleaching green next to a linen mill in Ulster around 1840.

Role of the Potato

This rickety system held together only because the rural peasants had a cheap and plentiful source of food. The potato, introduced to Ireland about 1590, could grow in the poorest conditions, with very little labour. The seed potatoes only needed to be laid on spade-dug beds, called 'lazy-beds', and covered with earth. This was very important, because labourers had to give most of their time to the farmers they worked for, and had very little time for their own crops.

Planted in April/May, the early potato crop would come into season in late August, and the potatoes would be stored in pits until the following May. The summer was therefore a time of some hardship, because families had to buy expensive oatmeal to eat until the new potato crop came in. If they could not afford oatmeal, they would travel the roads begging, to buy food for the 'summer hunger'.

There is no doubt that this easily-grown, vitamin-packed food assisted the enormous growth of population which took place in the early nineteenth century — Ireland had had just over three million people in 1800, but this had risen to about eight million in 1845. Even a small plot of land could support a large family, if you grew potatoes. An acre and a half would feed five or six people for six months, and an average adult male would eat 12 to 14 pounds (5-6 kilos) per day. About one-third of the potato crop was used to feed pigs and other livestock. Anything else a farm produced, such as butter, bacon, poultry or eggs, was sold for money. Life expectancy was about 38 years for men, which compared quite well with the rest of Europe at the time, and the average male was two inches taller than the British average.

However, it was a source of concern to some authorities that people had nothing to fall back on *at all*, if the potato ever happened to fail. They were at rock-bottom as it was.

Vignettes of Irish rural life around 1840

Unfortunately, this fear was not taken very seriously. There had been occasional local crop failures, but the crop always came back the next year. A major famine in the years 1739-41 killed thousands, including possibly one-fifth of the population of Munster. Famines had also occurred in 1816-17, 1822, 1826 and 1831, causing large numbers of deaths from starvation and fever, but small-scale aid was usually made available fairly quickly, through a mixture of government help and private charity. Local relief committees would be established, and relief works set up, on a short-term basis.

Under pressure to produce as many potatoes as possible, farmers gradually moved from the stronger types to one called the 'lumper' or 'horse potato'. This could grow on the poorest land of all, and gave a large crop. It had originally been developed as a food for animals, and was very soft and watery, with less vitamin content than other types. It was immune to diseases that attacked other potatoes, such as 'dry rot' or 'taint'. Fatally, however, it had no resistance at all to the immediate cause of the Great Famine, the fungal disease called 'blight' (*phythophthora infestans*).

Coming of the Blight

In June 1845, reports began to come from Europe that a new blight had been noticed in Belgium. It is not known for certain where it came from, but it had been in America since 1843, and may have been imported with guano (fertiliser) from South America. It spread into France, Germany, the Netherlands, Switzerland and England, and caused huge crop failures, in which thousands of people died. In these countries people were less dependent on the potato as a food, and a severe drought in Europe in 1846 helped to kill the blight there completely, so the effects were less catastrophic than in Ireland.

Scientists could not agree what caused the potatoes to rot and turn black. They blamed the cold weather, or insects, or some poisonous 'miasma' in the air. However, it was later found to be a fungus, with its spores carried on the wind. If the spores were buried in the pits where potato crops were stored, they would spread again when the new seed potatoes were planted in spring. All kinds of cures were put forward, but it was forty years before a fungicidal spray was developed against this potato blight.

On September 13, 1845, the *Gardeners' Chronicle* wrote, 'We stop the Press with very great regret to announce that the potato Murrain has unequivocally declared itself in Ireland... Where will Ireland be in the event of a universal potato rot?'

The police were ordered to keep records of the spread of the blight, and from these we can see that the worst affected counties in this first year were Waterford, Antrim, Clare and Monaghan. However, damage was slight, because the early crop had been lifted already. Less than one-third of the crop was lost, though even this was bad. The worst was yet to come.

Late in the afternoon, they had all the oats packed into bags, while
the empty sheaves were divided into two stacks, the light straw for
thatching the house and barn, the heavier straw for cattle feed and
for bedding. They were about to return to the house when Martin
sniffed the air and said:

'That's queer.'

'What is it?' the old man said.

'That smell,' said Martin. 'Can't you smell something queer?'

'Ga! Brother,' said Tommy sniffing, 'I smell something, but
maybe it's my own breath after yesterday.'

'Blood an' ouns!' said the old man. 'Would it be the blight?
Where is it coming from?'

'From up there,' said Martin, pointing towards the north, from
which a faint breeze was blowing. 'Phew! It's stinking. It's from
Patch Hernon's share up there. Look. There are people looking over
a wall into his garden.'

They all looked at the garden towards which he pointed. The
sun's rays now came slantwise through a gap between two high peaks
on the west, gilding the sombre Valley with a gorgeous light. The
vast shadows of the mountains made a ghostly pattern of
extraordinary beauty. Now the dim colours of the gorse, the heather
and the decaying green of the potato stalks were brought forth. The
white walls and faded thatch of the cabins that stretched in a crooked
row from where they stood to the Valley's end, above the western
bank of the stream, all shone in the brilliant evening light. Even the
parched grass and the stubble of the shorn oat fields stood out
distinctly against the solemn darkness of the unlighted mountain
caverns. Down below, the roaring torrent cascaded from the Black
Lake through narrow, rocky gorges, until it widened below the
house to a deep pool that was now yellow and turbulent with a press
of water, its banks fringed with a swirling rime of froth and jetsam
gathered by the flood.

'It's Patch Hernon's share sure enough,' said Martin. 'I'll go up
and see what's wrong.'

'Whist!' said the old man, 'Don't you hear?'

The sound of a woman's wailing reached their ears.

Having, I confess, lost many sleepless hours respecting the *cause* and *effect* of the **Rot in the Potato crop**, it struck me to try if I could find out the first, and alleviate the latter, no person *now* can be called an *alarmist*, who says that few fields in the kingdom have entirely escaped the contagion, and it is the Duty, as it should be the inclination of every one to state what they feel would be a remedy for the evil. I gave up an entire day to trying experiments upon the *diseased Potatoes alone*. I got the full of a middle sized Pot of them peeled and boiled well, as soon as they come to a boil, I had the first water thrown off, cold water put on, and on the second water being put off, (having previously boiled two salt herrings, the bones taken out,) added them and had all *well pounded* together put in a small quantity of ground pepper and a little salt, I then sent for my Labourers twelve in number I first, myself, tasted it, and made each of them do so, they all pronounced it *"very good"* and some eat heartily of it, all declaring they would persue the plan and expressed themselves most thankful, I had a pot of Potatoes put down in the usual way with the skins on excepting the rotten part, and as before the first water being thrown off (which had such a bad smell, I would not allow it to be given to the pigs) and cold water added, *on the top* I put three salt herrings and boiled them on the Potatoes, and all being turned out in the usual way on the Riddle and the Herrings put on a plate in the middle, the family sat down to dinner, and I give their words "only for the Herrings these Potatoes we could not eat", I divided a Barrel of Herrings among those Labouring Tenants according* to the number of their familes from 90 to 120 each, and gave to each a paper of pepper, I gave Tin Graters to them for making starch, which I found the women *understood perfectly*, and I was happy to see some begining to be used before I left them, I would be very glad to be able to state the result of these tryals, but am anxious to make those which I have made public, feeling that no time should be lost, not even a day, in giving these first results, and I say to all others, "what you do do quickly" remember there are 9 months to come before a new crop can relieve, and all that can, should be done to make the present beneficial both for feeding and Seed.

Richmond, Dundalk,
October 23rd, 1845.   LENNOX BIGGER

*NOTE.—I have ordered tryals to be made with mixing a Turnip or two to the champ and 2 or 3 onions in others. I intend also to try the starch which a gentlemen stated would give 3lb of flour from the stone of Potatoes, 24lb from the Cwt. would be very valuable for rotted ones, would be 4s. per Cwt. at 2d. per lb.
The Barrel to get is what contains 9 Hundred, some (large) have only 6 cwt. The tin grater, a sheet tin cost 4d.

Above: Many suggestions were made for use of diseased potatoes. Most were too expensive to be practical, or assumed the diseased crop was still nourishing.
Below: Printed notice describing in Irish and English how to make ventilated pits. These attempts to preserve the diseased crop failed.

Paint don' lic̄ir fir Seaƺailre 'ran Iantar.

Cum cunƺnaṁ a tabairt dona huilib a mbeiƺ ciocṗaċ cum na llaiṁ a ċuir air an obair, tairbeaureaḋ me roium na bpoll map d'oroṁƺear a mbeiċ deanta; 7 b-reidir ƺo mbeiċ an pictuire rir urardeaiċ doib:—

<table>
<tr><td>( )</td><td>Poll-ƺaoiċe.</td><td>( )</td></tr>
</table>

Toƺ ionaḋ tirin rpeariuiril don bpoll. Aƺ rin dean poll-ƺaoiċe leatan ƺo leor, air banna na caliṁan, a broirin ċuirre orƺuilce no abroirin liuceire, le ƺeauaḋ ċuirre naoi norluiƺe no choiƺ air leaċat 7 air doiṁueaċ, 7 le cuir mion cloċ air a dcrearna air. Tarraiƺ an ċuirre no an liuceirere air raḋ an poill 7 raƺ orƺuilce 'na ḋa ċeann e, ionur ƺo nƺeabaċ an ƺaoċ ċriḋ ƺo caorƺa. Cuir na ƺaoiċe a ƺabail nior reap (an niḋ ir nior miocḋanaiċe,) dean poill-ƺaoiċe a

---

Extract from the Letter of a " Western Rector."

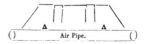

To assist all who may be desirous to lay their hands to the work, I shall describe the pits as I have directed them to be formed; and perhaps the subjoined diagram may aid them :—

<table>
<tr><td>( )</td><td>Air Pipe.</td><td>( )</td></tr>
</table>

Let a dry and airy site be chosen for the pit; then let an air-pipe or funnel be made, of tolerable width, either on the surface of the ground, in form of a French drain, or in that of a lintern, by cutting a trench nine inches or a foot in depth and breadth, and laying stones loosely across it; and let this funnel be carried the whole intended length of the pit, and left open at both ends, freely to admit the air. To render the ventilation—and ventilation is the great desideratum—still more complete,

Extract from Constabulary report on the state of the potato crop in 1845

Donegal	Carndonagh	Nov 12	The disease is increasing fast, particularly in the pits. The farmers are generally trying the suggestions of the Commissioners.
Kildare	Kildare	13	Since the fall of rain, the crop is rapidly running to decay. The poorer class of people are beginning to despair.
Tipp S.R.	Tipperary	12	The disease has spread extensively in the pits, a large portion of the potatoes pitted as sound 3 or 4 weeks ago being now bad and in some instances *unfit for any use*. On the lowest calculation, one third of the entire crop is diseased: & though the produce of this season is considered to be from 1/6 to 1/7 greater than that of last year, there must be a great deficiency. The people seem very regardless of the advice circulated — more particularly the poorer class whose crops are the most affected.

Donegal Carndonagh 12 The disease is increasing fast, particularly in the pits. The farmers are generally trying the suggestions of the Commissioners.

Kildare Kildare 13 Since the fall of rain, the crop is rapidly running to decay. The poorer class of people are beginning to despair.

Monaghan Glanslagh 13 The state of the crop is much the same as on 6th instant. The people only dig what they require for present use, thinking that the potatoes will keep better in the ground. The greater part of the injury to the crop appears to have occurred between 24th Sept. & 14th October. — With very few exceptions the inhabitants of this district pay no attention to the Commissioners' Instructions, which have in many instances been torn down or

CHAPTER 2

1845-46

Early Relief Efforts

By the end of 1845, it was obvious that the blight was spreading around Ireland. A group of concerned citizens in Dublin established a committee (The Mansion House Committee) to appeal to the British government for some kind of help. They received letters from all over the country, prophesying disaster, and giving details of the devastation. Potatoes were rotting in the ground, and the ones already in storage were 'melting away'. One writer confessed that his heart trembled when he thought of the future that might lie before them.

At this stage the blight, although unexpectedly widespread, was being thought of as a once-off event, with the crop coming back to normal the following year — this had often happened before. The Mansion House Committee, appealing for aid, were naturally thinking in the short term. No-one could imagine that the need for aid would increase year by year for the next four years, decimating the population and draining a reluctant Britain of enormous sums of money.

The Act of Union, passed in 1800, had abolished the independent Irish Parliament in Dublin, and brought Irish administration under the British Parliament. The Irish administrative system was based in Dublin Castle, but supervised from London. Isaac Butt, a prominent Irish Member of Parliament, complained later that Ireland had been promised great things from the Act of Union, with all the advantages of being linked closely to a great and prosperous nation. Ireland was now about to learn just how close (or otherwise) that link was.

The dominant economic theory in mid-nineteenth century Britain was *laissez-faire* (meaning 'let be'), which held that it was not a government's job to provide aid for its citizens, or to interfere with the free market of goods or trade. This has to be remembered, because otherwise a lot of the Government's attitudes to the disaster in Ireland do not make sense.

People were supposed to be self-sufficient, and the attitude of the state was that to give them charity would

'Destitution in Ireland: Failure of the potato crop', Pictorial Times, 22 August 1846

To those who have never watched the progress of protracted hunger, it might be proper to say, that persons will live for months, and pass through different stages, and life will struggle on to maintain her lawful hold, if occasional scanty supplies are given, till the walking skeleton becomes in a state of inanity — he sees you not, he heeds you not, neither does he beg. The first stage is somewhat clamorous — will not easily be put off; the next is patient, passive stupidity; and the last is idiocy. In the second stage, they will stand at a window for hours, without asking charity, giving a vacant stare, and not until peremptorily driven away will they move. In the last state, the head bends forward, and they walk with long strides, and pass you unheedingly.

Asenath Nicholson was an American woman who travelled throughout Ireland with Bibles in Irish and English for distribution among the people.

weaken their ability to look after themselves. The most that was provided was the Poor Law (1838), which aimed to provide accommodation for the absolutely destitute in workhouses. These were administered by Boards of Guardians, and there were 123 of them in Ireland in 1845.

However, the conditions for entry were so strict that people would only go to them as a last resort. Families were torn apart, as women and men lived in different parts of the workhouse, and children were kept separately from adults. Inmates were forbidden to leave, and the food provided consisted of two meals a day, of oatmeal, potatoes and buttermilk.

There were strict rules against bad language, alcohol, laziness, malingering and disobedience, and meals had to be eaten in silence. Able-bodied adults had to work, at such jobs as knitting (for women) and breaking stones (for men). Children could be given industrial training of some sort. The aim was to give the least amount of help possible, and to discourage people from claiming what little there was.

The British government was also inclined to feel that landlords who had property in Ireland should be the ones to look after their tenants, instead of leaving it to the state. Some landlords did so, and indeed many were beggared by the help they provided during the Famine. But most of them did not care, and were only anxious to make what profit they could from the situation, either by claiming state aid or by clearing their tenants from the land.

Scientific Commission

The British Prime Minister, Sir Robert Peel, became concerned about the reports of blight in Ireland. One of his first reactions was to propose a Coercion Bill, to make sure that law and order did not break down. (This bill did not pass.) He then sent over a Scientific Commission (Sir Robert Kane, John Lindley and Lyon Playfair) to examine the facts. The commissioners reported that one-half of the crop was now destroyed, or unfit for use. Actually, this was an exaggeration, because enough remained to tide people over until the next crop, and there was no reason then to think this wouldn't be back to normal. They diagnosed the disease as some sort of 'wet rot', which was inaccurate.

Food prices in Ireland were beginning to rise, and potato prices had doubled by December 1845. Meanwhile, the Irish grain crop was being exported to Britain, as usual. The Irish market was small, and could not afford high prices, and the traders wanted their profits. Public meetings were held, and prominent citizens called for the exports to be stopped and for grain to be imported as well. However, this would have meant repealing the Corn Laws, and there was great opposition in Britain to this.

The Corn Laws, an exception to the doctrine of *laissez-faire*, laid down that large taxes had to be paid on any foreign crops brought into Britain. This kept grain prices high, and the British traders would lose profits if the laws were repealed. But Peel knew that only large imports of corn from abroad could help a widespread famine in Ireland.

The rest of his party, the Conservatives (or Tories), were opposed to interference with market forces, and Peel had to resign as Prime Minister in December, saying 'Good God, are you to sit in cabinet, and consider and calculate how much diarrhoea, and bloody flux, and dysentery, a people can bear before it becomes necessary for you to provide them with food?' He had been Chief Secretary in Ireland during the famine of 1816-17, and had forgotten nothing of it.

The opposition party, the Whigs (Liberals), were in favour of ending the Corn Laws, but their leader, Lord John Russell, was unable to form a cabinet because of disagreements within the party. Peel became Prime Minister again, and forced through the repeal of the Corn Laws in June 1846.

Purchase of Indian Corn

Unknown to his party, Peel had in fact secretly arranged, in November 1845, to purchase £100,000 worth of Indian corn (or maize) from America, in the hope of preventing some of the distress in Ireland. His intentions were good, but Indian corn was not the most efficient substitute for potatoes — it was very hard to mill (the Irish had few mills), it was difficult to digest, and people who were used to the bulk of potato in the stomach were left unsatisfied by Indian corn. However, there was no existing British trade in it (it was almost unknown in Britain), so it was not affected by the Corn Laws.

> Excellency may order that an emmediate
> Supply of Indian Corn meal be
> sont to this district, and sold to us at
> Rices our Wages can reach.

marks of
memorialists

twell
8 1846

Thomas Mollowney (Rue)—✗   5 in family
Thomas Ford ————   ✝ 7 — " —
John Huse ———— ✝ 8 — " —
Mical Burans   ✗ 8 ———
Ricke Burans —— ✝ 6 ———
Patt Canon ———— ✗ 7 —
Wiliam Cannon ———✗ ✗ 4. —
Patt Gualish ———— ✗ 10. —
Alic Fohy ———— ✗ 7.
John Morony — — — ✝ 7
John Gilins — — —. ✝ 8

William Steuart Trench

On August 6, 1846, — I shall not readily forget the day, — I rode up, as usual, to my mountain property, and my feelings may be imagined when, before I saw the crop, I smelt the fearful stench, now so well known and recognised as the death-sign of each field of potatoes. I was dismayed indeed, but I rode on: and, as I wound down the newly engineered road, running through the heart of the farm ... I could scarcely bear the fearful and strange smell, which came up so rank from the luxuriant crop then growing all around; no perceptible change, except the smell, had as yet come upon the apparent prosperity of the deceitfully luxuriant stalks, but the experience of the past few days taught me that all was gone, and the crop was utterly worthless.

William Steuart Trench was a land agent in Kerry. This piece refers to his own property in his home county of Laois.

To his Excellency Lord Heytesbury,
the Lord Lieutenant and Governor General of Ireland.

The humble petition of the farm labourers

residents in the parish of Killeeneen, Barony of Dunkellon and County of Galway.

Sheweth

That the price of potatoes in the district is over five pence per stone*. That a days wages, without food and now in the busiest season, is eight pence.

That many of us have wives and families — the number in each family is placed opposite our names herento affixed: that a stone of potatoes is the allowance to daily support one man, that some of us having families require two stones, others require three stones daily. That manifestly our wages and with constant employment, would not enable us to feed ourselves and families: that our potatoes are nearly run out, with some of us already exhausted.

That year after year we see wages having a tendency to fall lower and lower: that from the abundance of labourers, the rate of wages is kept down, whilst the price of food rises from scarcity and other causes: That annually new mouths are added and fresh hands from boyhood are able to join us, encreasing our numbers, still the land, that is the source of our food, is the same in quantity.

That we feel our remedy is cheap food, so as to bring the price along side the rate of wages; because, if wages cannot keep up to the price of food, food should keep pace in price with the rate of wages, — for, wages is the measure of food to feed the labourer: if not, the labourer would be cut out of his share of the fruits of the Earth.

That we have heard that Indian corn meal, from foreign parts, has been brought over to this country by the Government, and to be sold at such prices as would enable poor men (earning *free* wages and obliged to buy *protected* price food, and now encreased in price from the failure of the potato crop) to feed themselves & families: That we seek no charity, we only want to get enough of food in exchange for all we can obtain by hard and honest labour: we ask our measure of food, that wages merely represents. That we want no relief by Poor Laws — that the whole world beholds our distress, and yet these laws require (us) to prove our distress, ere aid be afforded, by submitting to imprisonment and separation from our wives and children; and where are the work houses to hold our numbers.

That we never before petitioned Government to look to us: that we do so now, because we are assured our necessities shall be cared for.

Petitioners humbly pray that your Excellency may order that an immediate supply of Indian Corn Meal be sent to this district and sold to us at prices our wages can reach.

Craughwell

April 13th 1846

*The petition was marked by 81 labourers (in place of a signature), and the number in each family given. (*A stone is 14 pounds, or 6.4kg approx.)*

A famine burying-ground on the sea-coast has some peculiarities belonging to itself. First, it often lies on the borders of the sea, without any wall, and the dead are put into the earth without a coffin, so many piles on piles that the top one often can be seen through the thin covering; loose stones are placed over, but the dogs can easily put these aside, and tear away the loose dirt. This burial-place was on a cliff, whose sides were covered with rough stones, and the ascent in some parts very difficult ... A straw rope was lying near a fresh-dug grave, which the pilot said belonged to an old man, who two days before he saw climbing the cliff, with a son of fifteen lashed to his back by that cord, bringing in his feeble hand a spade.

'I untied the cord, took the corpse from the father's back, and with the spade, as well as I could, made a grave and put in the boy'; adding, 'Here you see so many have been buried that I could not cover him well.' This was the burial-place of Arranmore, and here at the foot was the old roaring ocean, dashing its proud waves, embracing in its broad arms this trembling green gem, while the spray was continually sprinkling its salt tears upon its once fair cheek, as if weeping over a desolation that it could not repair. At a little distance was a smooth green field, rearing its pretty crop of young barley, whose heads were full and fast ripening for the sickle. 'This,' said Mr Griffith, 'is the growth of seed which was presented by William Bennet, last March, the poor creatures have sowed it, and if the hands that planted it live to reap the crop, they will have a little bread. Take a few heads of it, and send them to him as a specimen of its fine growth, and of their care in cultivating it.' 'Had these industrious people,' he added, 'been supplied in the spring with seed of barley and turnips, they would not need charity from the public. The government sent a supply around the coast, the delighted people looked up with hope, when to their sad disappointment, this expected gift was offered at a price considerably higher than the market one, and we saw the ships sailing away, without leaving its contents; for not one was able to purchase a pound. And we have since been told, that the "lazy dogs" were offered seed, but refused, not willing to take the trouble to sow it.'

Indian corn was also extremely cheap. It became known as 'Peel's brimstone', partly because of its bright sulphur-yellow colour, and partly because of its effects on the digestive system.

Although it was unpopular at first, demand for it rose as the famine got worse. Because of the milling difficulty, later imports were of cornmeal rather than grain. It was also found that if you mixed it with oatmeal (one part to three) it was easier to eat and digest. Peel is said to have brought in as much as would feed 490,000 people for three months, at 1 pound in weight per head per day. This was exceptionally generous aid for the time, and was opposed by many in the government as excessive.

Relief Commission

Peel now created a Relief Commission, the first solution proposed to deal with what became the Great Famine. The Commission, which was to organise aid to Ireland, and get it distributed, was made up of representatives of the army, police, Poor Law Commissioners and the Dublin Castle administration. It was chaired by the highly-efficient Sir Randolph Routh, who belonged to the Army Commissariat. Sir Robert Kane, a distinguished scientist, was the one Catholic member. The Commission held its first meeting on 20 November 1845.

The aim of the Commission was to place food depots all over the country. They were not, however, to sell or distribute food, because this would affect trade and the traders' profits. They would sell the grain at cost price, to local relief committees, and these committees would sell it on to the local population, also at cost price.

The money for administering this system came, of course,

from the British Treasury. The Assistant Secretary of the Treasury, Charles Trevelyan, was to become a very important figure in the Irish Famine. He worked extremely hard to organise the relief schemes, but he was basically very unhappy with the whole idea of giving famine aid. Indeed, he tended to feel that the Famine was a punishment from God for an idle, ungrateful and rebellious country.

By August 1846 there were 648 local relief committees all over Ireland. They were run by county officials, Poor Law officers and local clergy, both Catholic and Protestant. As well as selling food aid, they were supposed to raise money locally to help the poor, and to set up some kind of employment. They found it very difficult to collect any money from the local landowners and ratepayers, and sometimes published lists of their subscribers to shame the non-payers.

The relief committees were answerable to the Relief Commission in Dublin, and it gave them grants in direct proportion to the amount of money they raised themselves. Food was only to be distributed according to the 'workhouse rule'. This meant that if there was any room at all in the local workhouse, food aid could not be given until it was full. However, this rule was broken more often than not, because there were only 100,000 workhouse places in the country as a whole, and there was no point in waiting. The committees were not meant to give away free food at all, but some did so in the poorest areas, where they found great distress. They could see that people were more and more unable to pay for food, and that some way of earning money would have to be provided for them.

Crowds beg for food outside a workhouse, while whole villages lie deserted, a witness to the numbers who left.

*Government sale of Indian Corn at Cork, Illustrated London News, 4 April 1846
Circular describing the establishment of the Killarney Relief Committee at a
meeting held in October 1845*

POTATO DISEASE.

PUBLIC MEETING IN KILLARNEY.

A Public Meeting of the Inhabitants of the Town and District of KILLARNEY, convened by requisition, " To take into consideration the state of the Potato Crop in this district, and to take steps to avert the calamitous consequences likely to follow the disease that now shows itself in that crop," was held on Saturday, 25th October, at the Court House, Killarney, when, on the motion of JOHN O'CONNELL, of Grena, Esq., J.P. ; seconded by JOHN COLTSMANN, of Flesk Castle, Esq :

HENRY ARTHUR HERBERT, of Muckross, Esq., J.P., and D.L., was invited to take the Chair, and ARTHUR LLOYD SAUNDERS, of Flesk, Esq., J.P., and B.L., to act as Secretary.

The Chairman having alluded to the objects for which the meeting was convened, read the substance of a letter he had received from Lord Kenmare, regretting his absence from the meeting, and expressing concurrence in any measures it might adopt or suggest, and stating that his Lordship had adopted certain regulations on his Estate to enable the easier purchase of Lime in small quantities for the preservation of the Potato Crop.

Proposed by MORGAN J. O'CONNELL, E-q., M.P. ; seconded by JOHN CRONIN, Esq., of The Park :

Francis Bland, of Woodlawn, Esq., J.P.
Maurice Brennan, of Sunday's Well, Esq.
Denis Coghlan, of Killarney, Esq.
John Coltsmann, of Flesk Castle, Esq.
Daniel Cronin, of the Park, Esq.
Daniel Cronin, jun., of the Park, Esq., J.P,
John Cronin, of the Park, Esq.
Denis D. Duggan, of Knocknaseed, Esq., J.P.
Henry Arthur Herbert, of Mackross, Esq., J.P., & D.L.
The Rev. Richard Herbert, of Cahirnane.
The Rev. Edward Herbert, Vicar of Killarney.
The Rev. Robert Hewson.
Denis Shine Lalor, of Castlelough, Esq.
John Leahy, jun., of Southhill, Esq., J.P., and B.L.
Henry Leahy, of Southhill, Esq.
Daniel Mahony, of Dunloe Castle, Esq., J.P.
Keane Mahony, of Cullina, Esq., J.P.
Denis M'Cartie, of Headfort, Esq. J.P.
Wm. Meredith, of Dicksgrove, Esq., J.P.
Richard Meredith, of Parkmore, Esq., J.P.
Daniel Moynihan, of Freemount, Esq.
Richard Murphy, of Killarney, Esq., J.P.
Dr. Murphy, of Killarney.
D. W. Murphy, of Killarney, Esq.
John O'Connell, of Grena, Esq., J.P.

The Great Hunger
Potato Famine in Ireland
1845-48

1,500,000 died of starvation & 1,000,000 emigrated—Irish Friends were entrusted with international relief funds to feed the starving, replenish seed & to redeem fishing nets & tools which had been pawned for food.

'The Great Hunger', from the Quaker Tapestry depicting the work of the Quakers since 1650. This Irish panel shows the relief work of the Friends during the Famine.

A family at the fireside painted by William Burke Kerwan in the 1840s. Kerwan was a Dublin artist who was later sentenced to transportation for life for the murder of his wife at Howth, in a controversial case in 1852.

Famine scenes: (above) *Another deserted village, and* (below) *The dying drag the dead, by Anne Therese Dillen.*

*'On the look out: a fisherman's wife and family waiting the return of the boats as
seen on the Killary strand, September 1841', by William Burke Kerwan*

Emigrants at Cork c. 1840. Among those who emigrated in the years before the Famine were some quite affluent people.

Above: *Annie Moore, aged 15, was the first person to pass through the Ellis Island immigrant reception centre in New York when it opened on 1 January 1892. This statue at Ellis Island is one of a pair by Jeanne Rynhart. The other is at Cobh, Co Cork.*

Overleaf, top: *the Departure of Queen Victoria from Kingstown Harbour (now Dún Laoghaire, Co Dublin), 10 August 1849. Engraving published by A. Lesage, Dublin.*
Bottom: *From the sketchbook of an unknown artist who travelled in the west of Ireland.*
Left, *Nora Dooday, Saturday 3 August 1850.*
Right, *Little Eliza Morrison in the orphan asylum at Mrs Kurx's near Crossmolina. The caption notes: 'What did they do to your mother in the poorhouse, Eliza?' 'They trampled on her and killed her, Sir.' 19 August 1850*

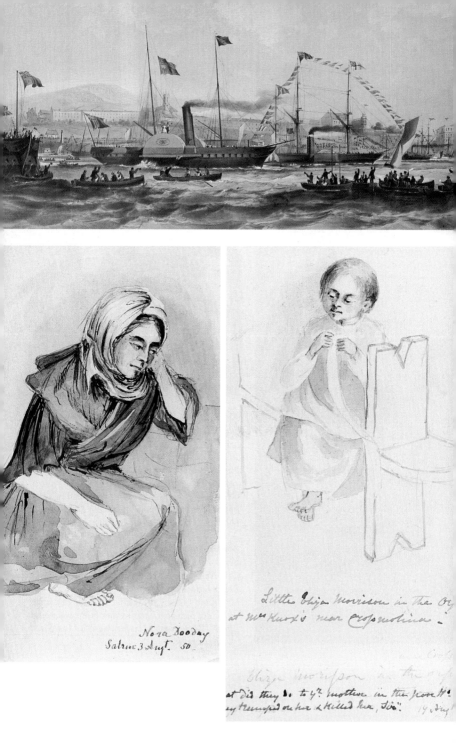

Nora Booday
Saturne 3 Aug.t 50

Little Elija Morrison in the O[...]
at Mrs Knox's near Crofsmolina —

Elija Morrison in the o[...]
at did they do to y.r mother in the [...]
[...]y trumped on her & killed her, Sir". 14 Aug.t

Top: *The Ulster-American Folk Park in Co Tyrone:
reconstruction of the type of vessel which brought
many Irish to America.*

Left: *A grave marker from the cemetery at Mission
Dolores, San Francisco. In the mid nineteenth
-century, San Francisco had a large Irish population
of Famine migrants. Three quarters of those buried
here are Irish, with birthplaces from Londonderry to
West Cork.*

Overleaf: *'Economic Pressure' by Seán Keating*

CHAPTER 3

1846

Relief Works

The Relief Commissioners began to discuss ideas for relief works, employing men to do such jobs as building public roads or drainage schemes or improving harbours. There was plenty of need for such improvements, but in the end the money provided went almost entirely to road-building, which was easiest to organise.

When Lord George Bentinck wanted railways built by relief works, he was told that private railway companies could not be supported by public money unless they could match the loan themselves, and that anyway railways were wanted only in prosperous areas, where there was less need for public works. Besides, if Irish railways were helped, English and Scottish ones would demand help as well. It was also true that two-thirds of the cost of building railways would go on materials, rather than labour.

Peel was depending on the local landowners to provide money towards his relief works, but he got very little from them. Some, indeed, did wish to support such works, but only if they could run them themselves, because they did not trust the efficiency of the local committees. Some landlords provided works on their estates, such as building towers or 'follies', or enlarging their boundary walls. Other landlords were holding on to their resources for the future, because they feared that worse distress was on the way.

Some of the relief works schemes were funded by the Treasury, through the local county administrations. This funding was supposed to be later repaid in full by each county (though in practice, very little of it was). Other relief schemes were run by the Board of Works, which had been established in 1831 to look after roads, bridges, harbours and fisheries. A county granted Board of Works aid would have to repay only half the grant, over twenty years. This was called the 'half-grant' scheme.

The half-grant scheme did not work as it should, because of local greed. Landowners and ratepayers saw a chance to attract money to their counties, at no immediate cost to themselves, and applications for relief schemes poured into the Board of Works. Many of these were from places which did not yet need help. By the end of May 1846, the exhausted and understaffed Board of Works had received applications which added up to £800,000 worth of works, and long delays were caused while they tried to sort them out.

The ordinary population, in the meantime, was having to wait, cruelly, for the relief works, which could not start without the Board's permission. People saw their only hope of food being delayed, and some rioting took place. Even when the works began, there were complaints of irregularities. Some committees gave work to people who didn't really need it, ignoring those in more desperate need. Some people who were given tickets, which gave them a place on the works, sold them for profit to whoever could pay them most.

Mill on the Awbeg river at Castletownroche, Co Cork, the scene of riots in November 1846, and below, Fermoy hospital, formerly a workhouse.

System of Payment

At first, wages were paid by the day rather than by the amount of work done. Farmers, who still needed work done on their farms, complained that this made the workers lazy, because they would try to make the job last as long as possible. The rates of pay were higher than the usual labourer's wage, and the nine or ten pence a day tempted farm workers to go to the relief works instead. The farmers were worried about future crops — what would happen if there was no-one willing to plough and sow?

There was a great shortage of currency in the economy, and relief committees who could not get hold of enough coin had to delay payments. An inquest on Denis McKennedy of Cork, who died in late 1846, found that he had died 'of starvation due to the gross negligence of the Board of Works'. He had not been paid for two weeks. His wife testified that the family of five had had nothing to eat all week but a few small potatoes, a head of cabbage and some flour, which she had got by selling turf. Dealers would sell food on credit, at exorbitant prices, to men waiting for their pay: some people will always profit from the distress of others. 'Gombeen men' or money lenders (often shopkeepers) became figures of hatred.

Crop fails again

These relief schemes were not always efficiently organised, but no-one had had experience of an aid operation of this size before. If matters had improved, the schemes would have begun to function more effectively, as a useful stop-gap before the new crop came in. However, in August 1846, all

How did the effects of famine generally show themselves?

The most fatal effects of starvation in the appearance of the poor people was a swelling about the face and a peculiar turn of the eye; the eye was made sharp and closed, and made long; the extremities of the feet became swollen, and the upper part of the feet less swollen; they were deformed; they were not well able to walk, and they became languid and careless about what became of them.

Evidence given by Rev. Meehan to the Poor Law Inquiry, 1849

hope of a short-lived famine disappeared. A rector in County Londonderry wrote, 'The entire crop that in the Month of July appeared so luxuriant, about the 15th of August manifested only blackened and withered stems. The whole atmosphere in the Month of September was tainted with the odour of the decaying potatoes.' The infected tubers from the previous year had been left in the fields, and had reinfected the new crop, because the mild winter had let the spores survive. The total yield of potatoes was enough to feed the population for just one month.

Lord John Russell, leader of the Whigs, became British Prime Minister in June, 1846, succeeding Peel. In terms of Famine policy, the new government was being threatened by the corn dealers about the import of grain to Ireland. They insisted that if the state continued to import grain, they themselves would refuse to. The government would then have to bear the whole burden of food supplies on its own. They were promised there would be no more state interference in their trade.

In fact, the government had been having difficulty in buying in grain supplies, because Europe was suffering widespread crop failures. Potatoes, rye, oats and barley were all in short supply, and prices were rising at speed. Britain itself was going through an industrial depression, and was

Asenath Nicholson
in Arranmore, Co Donegal

Six men, beside Mr Griffith, crossed with me in an open boat, and we landed, not buoyantly, upon the once pretty island. The first that called my attention was the death-like stillness — nothing of life was seen or heard, excepting occasionally a dog. These looked so unlike all others I had seen among the poor — I unwittingly said — 'How can the dogs look so fat and shining here, where there is no food for the people?' 'Shall I tell her?' said the pilot to Mr Griffith, not supposing that I heard him.

This was enough: if anything were wanting to make the horrors of a famine complete, this supplied the deficiency.

A Connemara Cabin, from the Illustrated London News, 1846

reluctant to spend too much on food aid for the neighbouring island.

The Whigs, afraid that the Irish were becoming too dependent on government aid, decided to close down the relief committees. They were still, of course, hoping that the August 1846 potato crop would be good. The Relief Commission thus ended its work on 15 August 1846, but reluctantly, fearing that the need for relief was not yet over.

Trevelyan, in the Treasury, was determined not to transfer famine from Ireland to England. It would not be fair, he said, for English and Scottish labourers to go without, or to have to pay higher food prices, for the sake of the Irish. He now directed the Board of Works to close down the relief works.

There was very little public protest from Ireland about this decision. The majority of the Irish Members of Parliament had supported the election of Russell as Prime Minister, and could not be seen to attack him so soon. These MPs included Daniel O'Connell, who had led the successful campaign for Catholic Emancipation in the 1820s, and the unsuccessful movement for the repeal of the Act of Union in the early 1840s.

Relief Works Continue

Food prices in Ireland rose higher and higher, and by November 1846 a labourer would have needed to earn twenty-one shillings per week to support an average family. However, even on the relief works, no man could earn more than six or eight shillings, and he and his family would become more and more undernourished.

By the end of 1846, over 390,000 people were employed building roads, often leading nowhere, often in deserted areas where no-one would ever need a road, anything just to keep the work available and the people alive. Over 150,000 people were still seeking such work, but could not get it, so were obviously in a state of severe distress — perhaps half a million were starving, when you consider that most of the applicants had dependent families.

The huge numbers flooding to the works, scrambling for a chance to earn a little money and willing to work up to ten hours a day, made for an administrative nightmare. Often people most in need failed to get work, because places were taken by farmers and their families who were in no such need, but knew someone on the local committee. In Corofin, County Clare, there were reported to be at least a hundred cases where a comfortable farmer was left on the list, while 'his neighbour, with nothing in the world but his spade and his limbs, has been struck off'.

Another and heartrending problem for the Board of Works officials was the numbers who applied for work, but were obviously so weakened by want that they could barely lift a shovel. How could they be turned away? In some cases women were employed, the only providers for the children who crouched by little fires of lighted turf by the road. There was no choice — you could only work or die. There were also the blind and the lame; those who could not get into the workhouse had nowhere to turn but the relief works.

Asenath Nicholson in Mayo,
Lights and Shades of Ireland

... A cabin was seen closed one day a little out of the town, when a man had the curiosity to open it, and in a dark corner he found a family of the father, mother, and two children, lying in close compact. The father was considerably decomposed; the mother, it appeared, had died last, and probably fastened the door, which was always the custom when all hope was extinguished, to get into the darkest corner and die, where passers-by could not see them. Such *family* scenes were quite common, and the cabin was generally pulled down upon them for a grave.

High pavement in Fermoy, Co Cork, created in 1846 by relief work labourers lowering the hill's severe gradient.

Left: Certificate entitling the holder to employment on public works. Under government regulations, only those holding these certificates from relief committees could be employed.

Threatening notices sent to landowners in Ballingarry, Co Tipperary in July 1846, to demand public works in the area. Transcript below.

Notice

I do hereby require of you to set on work in your neighbourhood or if you will not you will feel the displeasure of me and me brethren.

Captain Starlight

Notice

I do hereby require of you to set on work in your neighbourhood or if you will not I will not bear hunger no longer while there is beast in the field and i do Bleam you for the whole of it that you would not exert your self alike all the gentlemen in the Country I give you Three Days Notice When you are not a penny out of pocket it appears to me that you are Betraying the Neighbours

I am as well Die by the rope as Die by the hunger

When Trevelyan ordered the closure of the public works in July 1846, there was an outcry. They were obviously all that would prevent the deaths of thousands of people, and the risk of closing them was far too great. The Board of Works felt that there was still no guarantee that the new crop would be good, and refused to close them down. But Trevelyan was worried that the coming grain harvest would not be saved for lack of labourers, nor would enough turf be cut for the winter.

In the end the works were allowed to continue, and two special Commissioners, Richard Griffith and Thomas Larcom, were appointed to supervise them. They found the Dublin Board of Works offices crammed to bursting, the corridors filled with petitioners and desks piled high with applications. The authority of local committees to choose the workers was taken away. Now the committees were to draw up lists of eligible workers, and these would be checked by the Board.

The Board of Works was run very efficiently: 90% of its income went directly to pay the wages of the relief works, and very little was spent on bureaucracy. In December 1846, it spent £545,054, but by February 1847 this had risen to £944,141 for one month.

As the farmers continually complained, the relief works were distorting the labour market. Farmers could not, or would not, pay decent wages to their labourers, and had to watch more and more of them head for the relief works, abandoning their little patches of land because they could not work for the rent. Money wages had become essential for survival.

The system on the relief works was now changed to piece-work payment, with average earnings of one shilling (12 pence) per day. The piece-work system was more difficult to organise, so payments were delayed again. It was also more complicated for illiterate labourers to understand,

and they suspected cheating. There was great resistance to it, and overseers were assaulted and threatened in some places.

At the village of Clare Abbey, in County Clare, the head steward of the works was fired on with a blunderbuss, and wounded, in December. The Board of Works halted the relief works in retaliation, and the local people sank into despair. The local inspector, Captain Wynne, had to appeal to the board to reopen the works, describing the women and children scattered over the turnip fields looking for scraps while they shivered in rags in the snow.

It became obvious that even if the 1846 crop were healthy, there would not be enough of it to feed the population. They had been forced to eat their seed potatoes, and the government refused to buy and distribute seed, in case this created a dependence in future years. Even if they had agreed to do so, there was no way of transporting and distributing the huge amounts of seed necessary. The end result was that the 1847 potato crop, although it was not affected by blight, was only one-seventh of what it had been in 1846.

CHAPTER 4

1846

Food Supplies

What were people living on, if the little they could earn bought only as much grain as would keep them on the verge of life? Although tillage (growing crops) was the main form of agriculture, there were cattle farmers in Ireland too, and some sheep farmers. These were soon having to guard their herds from people who were desperate for food. The domestic pigs and chickens, of course, had long been eaten.

One form of nourishment used was the blood from cattle, baked with whatever vegetables were available. You could take a quart of blood (around 2 litres) from a cow without weakening it too much. Dogs, donkeys and horses were eaten and wild birds of every kind were trapped. It had been noticed before the famine that the overcrowding on the land had driven away much local wildlife such as foxes, hedgehogs, frogs and badgers, and any that were left now served as food. Nettles, dandelions, roots, mushrooms, berries and nuts were devoured. There were also small amounts of cabbage and turnips, and some herbs, the sort of food which prolonged life while destroying it.

It is always puzzling that fish were not more widely eaten, as they must surely have remained plentiful — Ireland is a country famous for its fish. However, sea fishing was a dangerous activity near the rocky Irish coasts, and was often prevented by bad weather. Harbours and piers were few and far between, and in poor condition. The boats used were 'currachs', wood and canvas rowboats which were too flimsy to go far from shore.

The fishermen tended to be as much dependent on their patch of potatoes as anyone else, and in fact as the Famine tightened its grip, they sold their nets and boats for any kind of food. They could eat shellfish and edible seaweed, of course, but supplies of these were soon exhausted. (Some desperate inland dwellers died from eating the wrong kind of shellfish, or dangerous types of seaweed.) A later report pointed out that the fishermen became too weak to row, and therefore ceased to fish. Also, the repair of their currachs needed supplies of tar and canvas every year, for which they could no longer pay.

An odd sidelight is provided by an account of the fishermen of the Claddagh, an isolated and close-knit community in Galway. The Quaker who visited them, seeking to help, complained that they would only go out at certain days and times, and if any fisherman from elsewhere tried to fish their waters, they would destroy his nets and beat up his crew. They would only collect enough fish for themselves, and would not let anyone else near it.

As for river fishing, for eels and trout, almost all the rivers belonged to landowners, and the poaching laws were apparently enforced as strictly as ever.

Labour Rate Act

In August 1846, when the government became aware that the new crop had failed and that things were only going to get worse, they decided to try another solution. They brought in the Labour Rate Act, which now put the complete cost of the relief works back to Ireland, to the local landowners and ratepayers. However, the costs would not have to be paid in full until later, and the landlords would not actually have to produce their own money up front. Tempted by this, hundreds of applications poured in to the Board of Works, and chaos ensued once again.

The Whigs also decided that, instead of reviving the system of relief committees, they would open food depots around the country. However, these were only to be opened in areas of greatest need, and to be used as a last resort. The areas nominated included Kerry, Donegal, West Cork, and the west of Ireland in general. New local committees were to be formed from the local gentry and county officials. The committees excluded Catholic priests from membership, even though these were the men who knew most about the local population.

Captain Arthur Kennedy, Kilrush, Co Clare

Eight sheep, the property of the parish priest at Carrigaholt, were lately killed and consumed in the neighbourhood of Tullig, where a number of evicted poor still linger. The owner refused to take any step towards prosecuting the offenders, as he informed me that he believed them to be in a state of starvation, and only hoped God would forgive them as freely as he did ....

Captain A.E. Kennedy was a Poor Law Inspector who gave this report to the Poor Law Commissioners

Top: Illustrations by Daniel Maclise to Moore's Irish Melodies, (London 1846)

Left: Punch cartoon from 1846.
The caption reads, Height of Impudence: Irishman to John Bull — 'Spare a thrifle, yer Honour, for a poor Irish lad to buy a bit of —— a blunderbuss with'.

Crime and Punishment

As news of the 1846 crop failure spread, people erupted in anger and despair. Crowds gathered in villages and towns, frightening the authorities and howling for work and food. They were usually dispersed fairly easily by armed soldiers, as they were weak and sick. The earliest demonstration seems to have been in Westport, County Mayo, on 22 August, when hundreds marched to the house of Lord Sligo. Another huge march took place in Macroom, County Cork, and a later one in Killarney, County Kerry.

These angry gatherings were being driven to protest by the sight of their families slowly withering away for lack of food, but they did not want to start a revolution, or to break the law — they just wanted help. However, there had always been small secret societies in Ireland, hoping for a social revolution, and they now saw a chance to make use of this despair and demoralisation.

The police called all these groups 'Ribbonmen', and they operated through violence and intimidation. They would post up notices calling people to public meetings, hoping to start riots. However, the local priests worked continually against them, and usually prevented trouble starting. The main enemy of revolution, in fact, was the exhaustion and apathy which was noted by many observers, and is inseparable from slow starvation.

The rise in crime during the Famine, from 20,000 on trial in 1845 to nearly 39,000 in 1849, was mainly due to non-violent crimes against property, not against persons. The use of cash on the relief works brought money into areas where it was uncommon before, and increased the opportunities for robbery. The most common crime was theft, of food or clothing, but large numbers of those arrested died before they could be brought to trial.

The usual punishment at the time was transportation — convicted persons would be exiled abroad, to hard labour in Australia, and rarely returned. As the Famine worsened, people began to commit crimes deliberately so that they could be transported. However dreadful it might be, it could not be worse than dying of starvation or fever where they were.

Asenath Nicholson,
Lights and Shades of Ireland

A man had died from hunger, and his widow had gone into the ploughed field of her landlord to try to pick a few potatoes in the ridges which might be remaining since the harvest; she found a few — the landlord saw her — sent a magistrate to the cabin who found three children in a state of starvation and nothing in the cabin but the pot, which was over the fire. He demanded of her to show him the potatoes — she hesitated; he inquired what she had in the pot — she was silent; he looked in, and saw a dog, with the handful of potatoes she had gathered from the field. The sight of the wretched cabin, and still more, the despairing looks of the poor silent mother and the famished children, crouched in fear in a dark corner, so touched the heart of the magistrate, that he took the pot from the fire, bade the woman to follow him, and they went to the court-room together. He presented the pot, containing the dog and the handful of potatoes, to the astonished judge. He called the woman — interrogated her kindly. She told him they sat in their desolate cabin two entire days, without eating, before she killed the half-famished dog; that she did not think she was stealing, to glean after the harvest was gathered. The judge gave her three pounds from his own purse; told her when she had used that to come again to him.

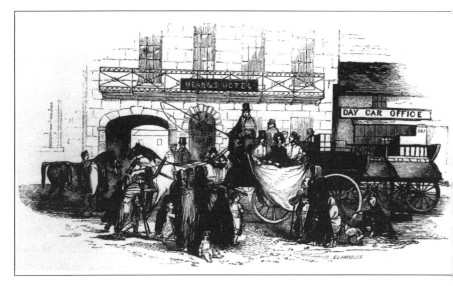

Above: Bianconi cars, public transport in 1841
Below: Carrying out the dead, lithograph by A. Maclure from Lord Dufferin and
G.F. Doyle, Narrative of a Journey from Oxford to Skibbereen during the
year of the Irish Famine, *published in Oxford in 1847.*

Terrible Accounts

By the end of 1846, newspapers were beginning to publish horrific accounts of hunger and death. Travellers came to Ireland to bring charity, and brought away vivid descriptions of conditions that seemed impossible in a civilised country in the western world. Specific towns were singled out as examples, such as Skibbereen and Schull, both in County Cork: '....in a few minutes I was surrounded by at least 200 of such phantoms, such frightful spectres as no man can describe. By far the greater number were delirious, either from famine or from fever. Their demoniac yells are still ringing in my ears, and their horrible images are fixed upon my brain...'

One writer described the inquest on a father of two very young children — his death had only been discovered when the children toddled into Schull, crying with hunger, and complaining that their father would not talk to them. The same writer viewed the body of a woman called Kate Barry, buried so lightly that she had been uncovered by dogs, and partly eaten. He thought he saw part of a horse's tail lying nearby, but discovered it was the skin and hair of her scalp. Thirty yards away, two wretched houses contained four dead bodies; although they had been dead a fortnight, they had not yet been buried.

Public opinion became agitated in Britain. This was, after all, supposed to be part of the United Kingdom. A good deal of charitable aid had already been sent, and it increased greatly under the influence of these descriptions. Magazines such as *The Illustrated London News* sent over artists who brought back graphic drawings of misery and deprivation.

This was Ireland, on the brink of 'Black Forty-Seven'. It would have been difficult to imagine that things could get any worse.

Clifden workhouse, Co Galway, in 1849, from the Illustrated London News

Report of Vice-Guardian to the Commissioners, Union of Loughrea, Co Galway

February 20, 1848 — Our first duty on arriving here was to visit the workhouse; and we can scarcely convey an idea of the total absence of any thing at all approaching to order or decency in which we found almost every department ... The probation wards... were in a very disreputable state, wet and filthy in the extreme; a heap of dirty straw piled up in one corner; several panes of glass broken in the windows, and their places supplied by pledgets of straw ... We found the adult paupers at breakfast. The Indian meal stirabout with which they were supplied was thin, much burned and otherwise infamously cooked. Many of the paupers were served with sour porter or beer (in lieu of milk) to take with their porridge; and on our inquiring the cause, were informed, that it had been sent by the milk contractor as his supply of milk was short... the portion of liquid (called milk) which he did supply, was in our opinion more than half water.

We found the kitchen department in a most unsatisfactory state; the boilers were in a disgraceful state of rust, totally unfit for culinary purposes ... Crowds of women in the day-rooms crouched in masses together round the walls, endeavouring to obtain warmth from the close contact with each other ... The dormitories were in a most irregular condition; the floors disgracefully disfigured, and in many places we fear approaching to decay, from the effects of urinal and other discharges continually taking place ... The pumps of the house are altogether out of order, and the pipes broken or otherwise destroyed; and the water required for the purposes of the house is carried in buckets from the lake by some of the female paupers, who were, when we first saw them, almost in a state of nudity.

CHAPTER 5

1847

Workhouses

Although the Famine had not yet reached its height, early 1847 saw the workhouse system beginning to collapse under the demands made on it. The Poor Law had been designed to deal with small numbers, not the catastrophe which now overwhelmed it. Workhouses all over Ireland were overflowing, and the death rate rose drastically. Standards of care, already low, collapsed completely. The food provided was often foul and rotten, but the slightest hope of food of any kind was enough to bring crowds to the gates of each workhouse, begging for admission.

By the end of February 1847, 116,000 people were getting workhouse relief, and 63,000 of these were children. Children provide some of the saddest stories of the Famine. Vast numbers were orphaned, of course, but many were deserted by parents who could no longer feed them, or who felt they had a better chance of survival in workhouse care.

The Poor Law authorities were continually on the watch

... There is no grass in England, not much in other parts of Ireland, and the turnips look very bad everywhere, they have not bulbed at all. This prevents the cattle jobbers from speculating. Our grass is fine, our turnips good, so by keeping our stock over we must be fully repaid by the high prices we shall get in the spring or may be at Christmas. In the meanwhile we get no cash and the rents may be uncertain. Some say this will be a harder year than the last. It is well the Colonel sold poor Major [a horse] or we certainly should be in a straight. £54. 10. 0d he got for him.

to see whether the children being left with them were really orphans, or had contact with families outside. But however hard they tried to prevent it, parents would leave the workhouse in the middle of the night, climbing through windows and over high walls, abandoning their children.

Hundreds of children were left behind by emigrating families, to follow on later, but never left the workhouse alive. Some lucky ones were reunited with their families, years later, but it was difficult to trace children in the workhouses. Those who were left there very young often forgot their surnames, or that they had parents still living. There was little hope now for the illegitimate children or foundlings, whom workhouses had always taken in; they had to take their chances with the rest.

Relief Works stopped

The winter of 1846-47 was the coldest in Ireland in living memory. Poverty in Ireland had always been helped by the mild climate and the availability of turf for fires, but the cold now became intense, and people had no energy to cut turf.

The extreme cold began to affect the relief works too. The

weather became too bad to work in, but people still had to be paid, or they would starve. Trevelyan suggested half-pay for each day on which work could not be done, but the Board of Works officials on the ground found it impossible to agree with him, and most continued to pay every worker in full whether the work could be done or not. Over that winter, £4,848,235 was spent on the relief works.

The numbers applying for work had swelled to unmanageable size. By January 1847, over 500,000 were employed, but up to 400,000 more would soon be seeking work. The Board of Works began to run out of money. It was also running out of work fit to be done by weakened, starving men (and sometimes women). It was not that people were idle — they were incapable, and the men organising the work were torn between feeling ashamed of the small jobs they were asking people to do, and equally ashamed that they were expecting any work at all from skeletal figures who could hardly stand upright.

The system could not continue as it was, and one official informed Trevelyan that as the relief works were no longer of any practical use, it would make more sense, and be cheaper in the long run, to distribute food freely instead of making people earn money to buy it with. The average wage of about one shilling a day went nowhere, because the most basic subsistence for a family now cost two or three shillings per day, and this was only for food, not clothes or housing. Trevelyan, casting about for ways to avert the looming calamity, began to consider the example of the Quakers and their soup kitchens.

Ration cards issued under the Soup Kitchen Act. Adults were entitled to one full ration per day, while children got a half-ration.

Charitable Aid

The plight of Ireland had by now attracted attention from charitable and religious groups. The 'British Association for the relief of the extreme distress in the remote parishes of Ireland and Scotland' had collected over £470,000, including £2,000 from Queen Victoria and £1,000 from Baron Lionel de Rothschild. It worked through the local relief committees, storing and distributing food supplies. Subscriptions came from countries as far away as India, Russia and Australia.

Another active group was the Society of Friends (or the Quakers), who formed a Central Relief Committee in Dublin to co-ordinate their activities. Close links with American and English Quakers helped them get food from abroad. They did not want to get involved in politics, by criticising the government, or to interfere with trade by distributing free food. The food they did supply was rice, so as not to cut across the grain trade. They aimed to help local communities to look after themselves, and they provided equipment for this, such as large boilers to make soup. They established soup kitchens in many areas, and also helped to develop fisheries, and to encourage new crops, such as flax. Other benefactors, such as Father Mathew in Cork (the Temperance Movement priest), set up soup kitchens as well.

The relief efforts of the Quakers have lived long in the Irish memory, probably because they had no axes to grind, and wanted only to help. There were no political or religious strings attached to their aid. They are remembered simply as kind, generous, compassionate and efficient, and travelled tirelessly, often to areas where no-one else would go.

The society of St Vincent de Paul was set up to alleviate poverty, involving local people in aid. One of the earliest groups began in Kilrush, County Clare, in March 1847. This lay Catholic organisation is still active in Ireland today.

Society of Friends soup kitchen in Cork, *Illustrated London News, 16 January 1847*
Constable's report of finding a fever-stricken family. Transcript on facing page.

Immediately, but being refused
admittance there they were
sent back to this place
& left on the cold road out
day time. the most part of
the night & than put in to
a shed. on the following
day. (Monday) I informed
Doctor Atkins. of the case
who gave a Certificate stating
the Poor Woman. had Fever
and was a fit object for the
Fever Hospital
The Revd. Mr. Malony & two
Catt Paisens recommended

in to it. I went through the
neighbours and got a few pence
to get nourishment for them
and also procured a nurse
tender to take care of them.
it is a very hard case that
there is no place to receive poor
persons of this description when
they fall on the public roads
& although I am well aware it
is no part of my duty to interfere
in such cases. Still every person
calls on me to keep the Doe like
the public passways clear of such
nuisances. there is 7 or 9 families
at present ill with fever in this
neighbourhood. Some of them in shops,

Co. of Wicklow
Aughrim, June 16 1847

I have to state that on the 11th inst. a travelling pauper named Honor Kerwin and her child dropped on the highway near Aughrim, both being ill with fever and lay on the side of the road till the following day when I reported the case to Jeremiah Tool the warden, who had them conveyed to Rathdrum Fever Hospital immediately. But being refused admittance there they were sent back to this place and left on the cross roads at Aughrim the most part of the night and then put in to a shed. On the following day (Monday) I informed Doctor Atkins of the case who gave a certificate stating the poor woman had fever and was a fit object for the Fever Hospital.

The Revd. Mr. Malony and two cess payers recommended them to the Fever Hospital also. These recommendations together with the warden's note was forwarded same day, with the poor woman, to Arklow Fever Hospital and (she) was also refused admittance there stating they should 'have been sent to Rathdrum' and had them conveyed back to Aughrim and left on the cross roads for a night to the great danger of the people of this neighbourhood.

On Tuesday myself and two of this party with some others of the neighbours procured timber and erected a shed and put the two sick persons in to it and went through the neighbours and got a few pence to get nourishment for them and also procured a nurse tender to take care of them. It is a very hard case that there is no place to remove poor persons of this description when they fall on the public roads and although I am well aware it is no part of my duty to interfere in such cases. Still every person calls on me to keep the public passways clear of such nuisances. There is 8 or 9 families at present ill with fever in this neighbourhood, some of them in sheds and no place to receive them. I hope you will see if there is any remedy to this state of things.

John Norris,
Constable

The Soup Kitchen Act

In February 1847 the government finally gave up hope of the relief works, and brought in the 'Act for the Temporary Relief of Destitute Persons in Ireland', also called the Soup Kitchen Act. Its main aim was to establish temporary feeding facilities instead of relief works. They were only to last until September, when it was hoped the new harvest would relieve the situation a bit. The second part of the act would then come into force, starting the Outdoor Relief system.

'Outdoor Relief' meant making help available to people through the Poor Law system, but without making them go into a workhouse. This was an obvious step to take, because there was just no room left in the workhouses, and indeed by now large numbers of people were too weak to travel towards them. Now the destitute poor could stay in their homes, and collect food. This was an enormous change in the way the Poor Law was meant to work, and it went against some of the strongest principles of the government, but they could see no alternative. They did not want to be held responsible for the huge number of deaths which would otherwise take place.

A new Relief Commission was set up in Dublin to administer the soup kitchens, chaired by Major-General Sir John Burgoyne, an army engineer. Sir Randolph Routh was again a member, along with representatives of Dublin Castle, the police, and the Poor Law Commissioners.

A small finance committee was set up in each of the 130 Poor Law Union districts. There were also district relief committees, whose areas of responsibility covered the electoral divisions of the Poor Law administration. There were almost 2,000 of these by the end, and where they were set up depended entirely on local effort and initiative. Some remote areas were never reached at all. It took quite a long time to get this system up and running, printing and distributing 10,000 account books and 3,000,000 ration tickets. Meanwhile, the relief works began to close down.

Some of the relief committees took their time setting up the new system of food distribution, and kept the relief works going as long as possible. They felt the soup kitchens would be degrading; people would have to queue in public to be fed, and would be made to feel they were receiving 'charity'. Besides, soup kitchens would also be more troublesome for the organisers on the ground. However, the new Commissioners insisted that from 20 March 1847 the numbers on the relief works were to be cut by 20 per cent, with a further ten per cent in April. By the last week of June, all but four per cent of the relief workers had been let go.

This meant that 209,000 labourers now had no work, and no income, but the free food distribution was still not in place everywhere. 2,730,000 persons were being relieved each day, but the total needing relief was about 3,165,000. Almost 15 per cent of those who were let go from the road works were still not being reached by the soup kitchens.

Angry crowds gathered in some areas, and marched on the relief works, demanding work and rejecting the idea of collecting food. Some of the new soup kitchens were destroyed, in despairing revolt.

The soup kitchen system, when it finally got going, worked reasonably well, although there were abuses. In some areas, far more people were listed as needing food than had actually ever lived there, so those areas got a disproportionate amount of food. Some of the food went to working farm labourers, because their employers pretended to sack them so they could claim it, but continued privately to employ them. The food aid, was of course, strictly supposed to go only to the infirm, the destitute unemployed, and destitute landholders.

Some of the rules were broken for good reasons. No matter how poor and desperate they were, many people avoided claiming food aid because of the shame of standing in line. The rules said that all able-bodied members of a family had to come to the soup kitchen before any of them could be fed, but in practice the local committees were often satisfied if just one member of each family came.

The soup being given out was called 'stirabout', a mixture of two-thirds Indian meal and one-third rice, cooked with water. Earlier food aid had been given out uncooked, because this was easier for the relief committees, and gave people the freedom to cook their own share as they wished.

However, the art of cooking had been very neglected in rural Ireland. People were used to cooking nothing but potatoes, which were extremely simple to prepare. Indian meal needed more careful preparation, and if people did not cook it properly, it could lead to stomach upsets and diarrhoea. The committees had also found that some people sold the uncooked meal for tobacco or tea, or for alcohol. Fathers were found to have sold it for drink, instead of bringing it back to their waiting families. If the soup kitchens gave out cooked food only, it could not be hoarded or sold on, so this now became the rule.

At first people were very reluctant to take cooked food, no matter how hungry they were. It was seen as disgraceful to have to stand in line, carrying a pot or a bowl, to wait for your number to be called. But soon the only food aid available was in cooked form. Apart from anything else, it was much cheaper to provide this way, costing about 2 pence per ration. Besides, the widespread sense of humiliation meant that fewer people claimed it; they were willing to starve first. And this meant that more savings were made.

Although the idea of soup kitchens was good, it depended on the food being of good quality, made from decent raw materials. However, many of the relief committees went for quantity instead of quality, and they provided soup with very little food value. The Relief Commissioners had said that the daily ration was to include 1 pound weight of meal or flour, or 1 pound of biscuit, or 1½ pounds of bread, for every person over nine years of age, with a half-ration for those under nine years old; or one quart (2 litres) of soup thickened with a portion of meal, along with a quarter ration of bread, biscuit or meal. This was hardly generous, but some local committees reduced even these amounts. Some soup was far too liquid, leading to diarrhoea, and scurvy broke out because of lack of vitamins.

Watch house in the old chapel yard in Skibbereen, Co Cork. This picture appeared in the Illustrated London News, 13 February 1847, with the following report from a local doctor.

'On my return home, I remembered that I had yet a visit to pay; having in the morning received a ticket to see six members of one family, named Barrett, who had been turned out of the cabin in which they lodged, in the neighbourhood of Old Chapelyard; and who had struggled to this burying-ground, and literally entombed themselves in a small watch-house that was built for the shelter of those who were engaged in guarding against exhumation by the doctors when more respect was paid to the dead than is at present the case. This shed is exactly seven feet long, by about six in breadth. By the side of the western wall is a long, newly made grave; by either gable are two of shorter dimensions, which have been recently tenanted; and near the hole that serves as a doorway is the last resting place of two or three children; in fact, this hut is surrounded by a rampart of human bones, which have accumulated to such a height that the threshold, which was originally on a level with the ground, is now two feet beneath it. In this horrible den, in the midst of a mass of human putrefaction, six individuals, males and females, labouring under most malignant fever, were huddled together, as closely as were the dead in the graves around.'

Journal of Elizabeth Smith: 1847

Sunday again — the 17th — I hardly know how the week has gone — not a creature has entered the house but the Doctor. We have been as quiet as possible, indeed the country generally is very dull; people are oppressed by this frightful amount of bankruptcies, almost everyone either themselves or their friends affected by some of these numerous failures. Then the winter prospects look very gloomy. The destitution is expected to be wider spread than last year for the very poor will be very nearly as ill off while the classes above which then relieved them are all this year in serious difficulties. No money anywhere; the little hoards of cash and goods all spent and nothing to replace either. The ministry says the land must support the people on it. Half the country having been left untilled for want of means to crop it while a million of money was squandered in destroying the roads*, much of it finding its way into pockets full enough before. The Queen has ordered the begging box to go round all the English churches for us! Sir J. Burgoyne, head of the Poor Law Commission writes to the Times newspaper! to entreat charitable subscriptions for the starving districts. Mr Trevelyan, the Secretary to the Treasury, sends this precious emanation forth to the publick with some little agenda of his own to the same tune. One would suppose stones were scarce in Ireland and her rivers dry when no one hoots such drivellers out of the country. We want no charity. We want a paternal government to look a little after our interests, to legislate for us *fairly*, to spend what we should have properly among us without jobbing, to teach us, and to keep a tight rein over idleness, recklessness, apathy. It is plain these people can't do it. We must begin and call again for Sir Robert Peel as we did some years ago, for the state of the Empire is unpromising.

* *Many of the road works were badly planned and organised, or left half-finished, leaving roads worse than they had been before.*

The internationally-renowned chef, Alexis Soyer of London, was commissioned to produce a soup recipe which would be cheap and nutritious. He assured the Commission that one gallon of his soup could be produced at a cost of £1. However, the *Lancet* (a medical journal) wrote: 'M. Soyer proposes to make soup of the following portions: Leg of beef, four ounces; dripping fat, two ounces; flour, eight ounces; brown sugar, half an ounce; water, *two gallons*. These items are exclusive of the onions, a few turnip parings, celery tops and a little salt...The above proportions give less than three ounces of solid nutriment to each quart of soup...'

Sir Henry Marsh, Queen Victoria's doctor, published a pamphlet which warned that a soft, semi-liquid diet was only good for children, or for adults recovering from illness. It was no good for a working labourer, who needed solid food which could be digested slowly. Even if a semi-liquid diet was very nutritious, it would not keep someone strong or healthy if it was digested too easily.

One of the most well-established legends of the Great Famine is 'souperism', meaning that people were only allowed the soup if they gave up the Catholic faith, and turned Protestant. However, this only seems to have applied to privately-run soup kitchens, which were organised by over-enthusiastic Protestants, and there were very few of them, found mainly in Connemara and West Kerry. These zealots would serve meat soup on Fridays (when Catholics were forbidden to eat meat), or refuse to give soup unless people came to a Protestant church or bible class. Starvation forced some people to pretend that they would give up Catholicism, but these forced 'conversions' did not last.

The relief committees worked miracles day after day, coping with scenes of intense distress and misery, being met every morning by crowds of thousands of people, those that had strength to walk. Men and women dropped dead where they stood, people fought and shrieked to get near the head of the line, the stronger snatched food from the weaker. Again the Quakers were among the most hard-working of the soup kitchen organisers, but they were beginning to feel overwhelmed. No matter how much anyone did, they were only scratching the surface of the need which existed.

There was one basic flaw in the Soup Kitchen Act, and in the later Outdoor Relief system. The money was supposed to come from local ratepayers, not from the government. But by this time it was almost impossible to collect rates anywhere in Ireland, and the local committees and Poor Law Unions were running up huge debts. The rates needed to run this new system would have to have been at least ten times larger than anything collected before, but already soldiers and police had had to be used to collect the Poor Rate in parts of Galway and Mayo. It was estimated that each shilling of rates had cost one pound to collect.

The Relief Commissioners ended the soup kitchen scheme in September 1847, in preparation for Outdoor Relief. At its peak the scheme had fed three million people each day, and had managed to reach most areas of need. The total cost was £1,725,000; great savings had been made when supplies of Indian corn and grain arrived in February and March, causing the price to fall dramatically (Indian corn went from £19 per ton in February to just under £8 a ton in August).

The government was pleased with the operation of the scheme, and it had in fact helped thousands to survive. Even the small quantities of food helped to strengthen people against disease. But it should have been kept going; the need for such food distribution was not over yet, and Outdoor Relief was not going to be adequate to the demands on it. It was also a tragedy that the public works were closed down just when the international food crisis had ended.

Food was beginning to reach Ireland in larger quantities, and food prices were falling. Meanwhile oats, wheatmeal

NOTICE.

I HEREBY give Notice to the LABOURERS and POOR HOUSEHOLDERS on LORD CALEDON'S ESTATE, that his LORDSHIP and LADY CALEDON have instructed me to open

THREE SOUP KITCHENS,

In convenient parts of his Lordship's property, to supply Soup and Bread at a very moderate price ; and that such will be ready for delivery *at Twelve o'Clock, on Monday, the 28th inst.*, at the following places, viz. :—

> **The Model Farm ;**
> **The Village of Dyan ; and at the**
> **House of J. Marshall, at Brantry Wood ;**

And will be continued every Day, at the same hour, until farther Notice (Sundays excepted).

    The Labourers employed at Drainage and other Works, can send their Children to the most convenient of the above places, for a supply of Soup, &c., which shall be sent to them hot in Covered Cans. And in order to encourage useful industry amongst the Children, I hereby offer a Premium of 2d. per Bushel, for Bruised or Pounded Whin Tops, properly prepared as food for Horses and Cows, delivered at any of the above-mentioned places.

    LORD CALEDON has desired his CARETAKERS to permit the Children to gather the Whin Tops on any grounds in his Lordship's possession, particularly in the large STOCK FARM OF KEDEW, and in the Plantations of DROMORE, DROMESS, and LISMULLYDOWN ; and I am sure the Tenantry will also encourage so useful an occupation at the present moment, when it is so desirable to use the strictest economy in the feeding of our Cattle.

HENRY L. PRENTICE,
AGENT.

N.B.—A Double supply of Food will be Cooked on Saturdays.

CALEDON, 19th December, 1846.   ARMAGH:—PRINTED BY J. M'WATTERS.

Notice issued to tenants of Lord Caledon in Co Tyrone announcing that soup kitchens were to be opened, and offering three pence per bushel for whin tops (collected from gorse bushes) properly prepared as food for horses and cows.

and barley were still being exported from Ireland, but imports were five times greater than exports. Lord John Russell, committed to Free Trade, was afraid of causing food shortages in England if grain supplies from Ireland were cut off. This was a time of financial crisis in Britain, and resources had to be used carefully.

LETTERS FROM BALTIMORE.

Baltimore, 1st month 27th, 1847.

Esteemed Friend
    JOSEPH BEWLEY,
    Enclosed thou wilt please find Alexander Brown and Son's draft for £50, a contribution from our little company in this city for the suffering poor in Ireland. Thou art aware that the number of Friends here is very small ; most of them are in very moderate circumstances, which will account for the small sum now forwarded. We wish you every encouragement in your work and labour of love. Please acknowledge the receipt of this.

Respectfully thy friend,
RICHARD H. THOMAS.

Baltimore, 25th February, 1847.

Messrs. JOSEPH BEWLEY, JAMES PERRY, THOMAS PIM, JUN., Dublin.
    Gentlemen,
    The Irishmen and citizens of Baltimore generally have heard with deep regret the great calamity that poor Ireland has been visited with, in the loss of her crops for two years in succession ; they have watched with anxious eyes its progress on the population of that devoted country, until it has assumed the form of famine.
    An all-wise power governs all things, and knoweth what is right ; but the wailings of the destitute and famishing can only be alleviated by the administration of food, to stay the hand of death.
    The situation of the people of Ireland has brought into action the benevolent and philanthropic citizens of Baltimore.
    At a public meeting held in this city a short time since, (at which the Honourable Jacob G. Davies, Mayor, presided,) it was resolved unanimously, to collect subscriptions in behalf of the suffering poor in Ireland. We have progressed well thus far. At a meeting of contributors to the fund, it was resolved—" That we remit to the Central Committee of Friends in Dublin the amount now on hand, to be by them distributed as in their judgment and wisdom they may deem best ;" believing that your committee will continue to exercise your kind, liberal, and philanthropic care over the distribution of this small amount, as you have done over that of greater magnitude.
    The amount has been contributed to by many hard-working Irishmen, who earn their bread by the sweat of their brow, and would like to know that its benefits should reach over as large a space of Ireland as you can possibly extend it to, without partiality to age, sex, or religion.

* Another letter was also received from Francis Jackson, containing a further remittance of £73 5s. 1d.

Letters to the Society of Friends Central Relief Committee in Dublin, who were financed largely by contributions from Quakers in Britain and the United States.

of men and women, with increasingly fewer children and old people, thronging around the workhouse gates and the soup kitchens. Many were so weak from hunger that they fainted when they got some food in their stomachs. Others failed to reach any place where they could be helped; bodies were found on the roads, in the ditches, under the trees. Their friends had no strength to bury them, and to a great extent no longer cared.

In February 1847 the village of Schull, in County Cork, was visited by Commander Caffyn, whose ship was delivering aid from the Society of Friends. He found that of the population of 18,000, three-quarters were living skeletons. 'I had read in the papers letters and accounts of this state of things, but I thought they must be highly coloured to attract sympathy; but there I saw the reality of the whole — no exaggeration, for it does not admit of it ... Never in my life have I seen such wholesale misery, nor could I have thought it so complete...I could tell you also of that which I could vouch for the truth of, but which I did not see myself, such as bodies half eaten by the rats; of two dogs last Wednesday being shot by Mr O'Callaghan whilst tearing a body to pieces... These are things which are of everyday occurrence.'

On 8 February 1847, three months before his death, Daniel O'Connell made his final speech in the House of Commons, appealing for aid for his country: 'Ireland is in your hands, in your power. If you do not save her, she cannot save herself. I solemnly call on you to recollect that I predict with the sincerest conviction that a quarter of her population will perish unless you come to her relief.'

The Outdoor Relief system now began to operate, as the soup kitchens closed down. It was laid down (in a new Poor Law Act) that the non-able-bodied poor could be given relief either in the workhouse or outside, keeping their homes. The Boards of Guardians would decide who would qualify. The

Oct. 10. Sunday. Little in the papers but failures. Cattle dealers in Dublin have gone and caused immense distress, in fact paralysed the markets; not an offer for a beast of any sort at any of the late fairs, Banks, merchants, brokers, agents, all are bankrupt in all places. John Robinson has lost seven thousand pounds by bad debts, trusting people who have failed to pay; he must pay the millers who sent him the flour he so imprudently parted with out of his former profits, his capital, and learn wisdom by this shake. He hopes to recover about half this sum when the affairs of some of these firms are wound up ....

able-bodied poor, meaning those who were still able to work, could also be relieved if they were unemployed and destitute, but only inside the workhouse. If the workhouse was full, or was infected with fever, the able-bodied could be granted relief outside for just two months, if they agreed to hard labour.

Trevelyan was hopeful that the British government could now begin to move away from having to provide famine relief. If the new system worked, it could be run entirely by Ireland, from Irish resources. He did not seem to have any idea of how poor Irish resources were, how difficult it was to collect any money, how great was the load of debt that each Poor Law Union was already carrying. The grain harvest of 1847 had been good, but although prices were dropping, fewer and fewer people had any money at all, or any hope of earning money. Nothing could take the place of a full, healthy crop of potatoes. But the British government was becoming increasingly impatient with the endless famine, and the constant financial drain.

An English Quaker, James Hack Tuke, toured the west of Ireland in 1847, and said that large parts of Connacht, and of counties Donegal, Kerry, Limerick and Clare, could never produce enough local rates to cover the cost of relief. The small farmers were destitute, and rent arrears grew higher

THE ABSENTEE.

Contemporary cartoon depicting an absentee Irish landlord at Naples confronted by the ghosts of Irish peasants

and higher. In many cases the burden of rates (10 shillings in the pound for Westport Union) made farmers decide to leave their land, and emigrate. Even the great landlords could not pay what they owed.

Lord Clarendon (appointed Lord Lieutenant of Ireland in June) estimated that the relief given must be costing at least £42,000 a week, but the largest amount of rates collected in any one month was £64,000. Many Unions became bankrupt. Outdoor Relief was more expensive than keeping people in the workhouse, so there were constant efforts to keep the lists small, crossing off names for the thinnest of reasons.

It was all very well for Lord John Russell to say that

landlords must be compelled to pay, but what if there was no landlord available? Large, impoverished districts all over Ireland had no landed proprietor, wrote Clarendon to the government; 'he is absent or in Chancery and the estate subdivided into infinitesimally small lots... What is to be done with these hordes? Improve them off the face of the earth, you will say, let them die ... but there is *a certain amount of responsibility* attaching to it'.

Irritated by the Unions' failure to cope with their huge loads of debt, the Poor Law Commissioners dissolved dozens of Boards of Guardians, and replaced them with vice-guardians. Inspectors were appointed to report on the competence and administration of the Poor Law Unions, but it was obvious that no tinkering with the system was going to be of any use. There were not enough financial resources in Ireland, by itself, to deal with the unimaginable scale of misery and distress which had been reached.

The main problem with the Poor Rate was that it was very localised. Each locality dealt only with the problems of its own area, and of course it was almost impossible for the poorest areas to produce any money at all. But the richer areas, which still had some money available, objected strongly to helping other Unions in difficulties. When Poor Law units were reorganised in 1849, ratepayers worked hard to make sure that the boundary areas would be fixed so that they themselves would not have to deal with notoriously poor localities.

The new Poor Law Act contained a 'quarter-acre clause' (the Gregory Clause), which insisted that tenants who occupied more than a quarter-acre of land could not be helped by the Poor Law. This meant that people needing help would have to give up whatever rights they had to land, and it helped the landlords to clear the paupers off their estates for good. It was the landlords who insisted on this clause; the government had not looked for it.

No winter ever opened upon us more gloomily. It bids fair to set in early and with unusual severity. Every newspaper brings large additions to the long list of bankrupts; the whole mercantile world is affected by the pressure on the money market. Banks have failed everywhere. Manufacturers, traders, brokers. We can sell nothing, and though a bountiful harvest has filled the country with cheap provisions, no one can buy. This in England, Scotland. The Highlands is much worse. What then must Ireland be, dying only. It is beyond ruin in the South and West. Here we shall get on better, we hope; it is the paradise of the green isle this Eastern coast of Wicklow. The Colonel received yesterday the first order on the Treasurer of the Board of Works for his drainage money, so he will set on thirty men at once; such a gleam of comfort. I have money to last ourselves till the pay comes again in the middle of next month, but I can't pay poor Miss Clerk her half year's salary. I have given her five pounds to account merely, so as I keep matters going I feel it will be all. The Colonel spends nothing, he sold his horse to help us; gave up the Deccan prize money he had intended to build the lodge with, and I have put off paying the girls the money borrowed from them last year. No word from my editors either on whom I reckoned for our school. Well, when things come to the worst they must mend.

Pressure on Workhouses

By this stage, fewer than 115,000 inmates could be accommodated in the workhouses, and the sick and the healthy were being thrown together in overcrowded conditions. In Fermoy workhouse, in County Cork, for example, nearly 24 per cent of those admitted between January and March 1847 died. Many sick people waited until they were near death before they went to the workhouse, in the hope of a proper burial.

The relief authorities made various improvements, such

The building we found most dilapidated, and fast advancing to ruin, everything out of repair, the yards undrained and filled, in common with the cesspools, by accumulations of filth — a violation of all sanitary requirements; fever and dysentery prevailing throughout the house, every ward filthy to a most noisome degree, evolving offensive effluvia; the paupers defectively clothed, and many of those recently admitted continuing in their own rags and impurity; classification and separation set at nought; a general absence of utensils and implements; the dietary not adhered to, and the food given in a half-cooked state — most inadequate, particularly for the sick; the meals distributed through the medium of one-sixth the number of vessels required, and uproar and confusion, the stronger securing an over quantity to the privation of the weaker, and the breakfast not completely dispensed until late in the evening; no contracts existing, no stores of provisions to meet even the wants of a day; the able-bodied not employed, and without restraint or discipline; the destruction of all description of Union property proceeding rapidly, many hundreds' pounds worth appearing to be missing; the children in the schools receiving no education or industrial training, in other respects their neglected state painfully exhibited by their diseased and emaciated aspect; no means for the proper treatment of the sick, the officers ignorant of their duties; coffins unused in the interment of the dead.

From a report sent to the Poor Law Commissioners

as building separate hospitals, expanding the space for accommodation, and freely giving Outdoor Relief even to the able-bodied poor. Workhouse places had tripled, to almost 309,000, by March 1851, but there was never any hope of having enough room for all those who needed help.

The local Boards of Guardians tried to restrict relief as much as possible, as they knew there would not be enough money to cover all the demands. In parts of Munster and Connacht, which had the highest number of paupers, the

Boards were terrified of being swamped by applications. The poor hated the workhouse system, and feared the fevers that were now spreading fast, so as many as possible applied for Outdoor Relief. By February 1848, over 445,000 people were receiving it. By the end of June 1848, this number had risen to almost 834,000.

Despairing scenes were common. 'Ranged by the side of the opposite wall [of Nenagh workhouse in County Tipperary], which afforded some shelter from the wind, were about twenty cars, each with its load of eight or ten human beings, some of them in the most dangerous stages of dysentery and fever, others cripples, and all, from debility, old age, or disease, unable to walk a dozen steps... In the evening some thirty or forty "paupers" were turned out to make room for an equal number of the crowd, while the rest returned weary and dispirited to the cheerless homes they left in the morning.'

One way of restricting Outdoor Relief was to insist on the paupers attending the workhouse every single day, to collect the cooked food offered. However, the Boards of Guardians often delegated the food distribution to meal contractors or shopkeepers, and this meant that there were far fewer points for distribution than there had been in the days of the soup kitchens. People had to walk several miles to the nearest point, and sometimes the food would have spoiled by the time they got home to their families. Poor health, bad weather, all helped to keep down the numbers who claimed their food. Eventually the fact was faced that cooked food caused more problems than it solved, and the authorities began to distribute uncooked food again.

Another effective way of keeping numbers down was the 'labour test'. The able-bodied poor were supposed to break stones for ten hours a day before they could be given Outdoor Relief. This was later lowered to eight hours. Stone-breaking was the most hated work that could be offered, and it kept many from claiming. But the 'quarter-acre clause' was the most efficient way of reducing the numbers on Outdoor Relief, as people resisted giving up their rights to the land they worked.

Reports from the south and west told the Relief Commissioners that landlords were abusing the clause in order to force smallholders off the land. The Commissioners could do nothing about these evictions, which placed further strain on the weak relief system. At the same time, reports showed that destitute smallholders were starving themselves and their families to death, rather than giving up their land. Eventually the 'quarter-acre clause' was relaxed for the wives and children of smallholders.

Conditions in the workhouses worsened daily, particularly for children. Dr Stephens, reporting on Cork workhouse in February 1847, found 150 boys in one ward, sharing twenty-four beds. The week before his visit, sixty children aged under thirteen had died in this workhouse. At Clifden, County Galway, James Hack Tuke wrote, 'I cannot easily forget the countenance of one poor lad about fourteen years of age who with a hollow choking voice begged of me a little meal to keep the life in him. The ghastly livid face and emaciated form wasted with hunger and sores of this breathing skeleton told me that to him this world would soon pass away.'

Even if the workhouse care had been good enough, most of the children arriving were already so weak and ill that hardly anything could be done for them. Reports from many workhouses all say the same things: '...the effect of the irreparable injury done their constitution previous to their admission...'; 'below the ordinary appearance of infant humanity...'; '...till I thus witnessed it I could not have believed how famine could clothe childhood with all the physical appearance of old age.' An English clergyman, Sidney Godolphin Osborne, wrote of Limerick workhouse:

Going out one cold day in a bleak waste on the coast, I met a pitiful old man in hunger and tatters, with a child on his back, almost entirely naked, and to appearance in the last stages of starvation; whether his naked legs had been scratched, or whether the cold had affected them I knew not, but the blood was in small streams in different places, and the sight was a horrid one. The old man was interrogated, why he took such an object into sight, upon the street, when he answered that he lived seven miles off, and was afraid the child would die in the cabin, with two little children he had left starving, and he had come to get the bit of meal, as it was the day he heard that the relief was giving out. The officer told him he had not time to enter his name on the book, and he was sent away in that condition; a penny or two was given him, for which he expressed the greatest gratitude; this was on Wednesday or Thursday. The case was mentioned to the officer, and he [was] entreated not to send such objects away, especially when the distance was so great.

The next Saturday, on my way from the house where the relieving-officer was stationed, we saw an old man creeping slowly in a bending posture upon the road, and the boy was requested to stop the car. The old man looked up and recognised me. It was he who had the child upon his back in the dreadful state. I did not know him, but his overwhelming thanks for the little that was given him that day, called to mind the circumstances; and, inquiring where the child was, he said the three were left in the cabin, and had not taken a 'sup nor a bit' since yesterday morning, and he was afraid some of them would be dead upon the hearth when he returned. The relieving-officer had told him to come on Saturday, and his name should be on the book, he had waited without scarcely eating a mouthful till then, and was so weak he could not carry the child, and had crept the seven miles to get the meal, and was sent away with a promise to wait till the next Tuesday, and come and have his name on the books. This poor man had not a penny nor a mouthful of food, and he said tremulously, 'I must go home and die on the hairth with the hungry ones.'

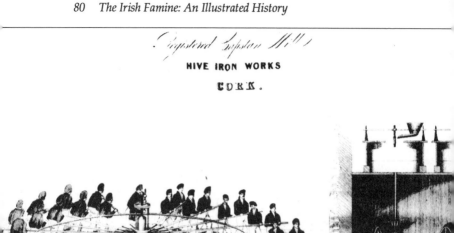

Registered Lupstan Mill

HIVE IRON WORKS

CORK.

Mill of the kind made for the Cork Union Workhouse, December 1848. The mill was used for grinding flour and meal and was operated by parties of forty men working for periods of two hours. It was designed for use in jails and workhouses.

'There was not the slightest evidence of even the least care being taken of them; as they filed before me two by two, they were a spectacle to fill any human heart with indignation.'

He described watching children die in the workhouses: 'I never saw one solitary instance of any one attempt to cheer these little ones, in any one of the very many ways in which we know children, sick and dying, can be cheered.' He was appalled by their lack of movement: 'in the very act of death still not a tear nor a cry. I have scarcely ever seen one try to change his or her position...two, three or four in a bed, there they lie and die, if suffering still ever silent, unmoved...'

In September 1847, Dunmanway Guardians sent six young children to Bandon workhouse, because they came from that area. The driver was given instructions to leave them outside the gates and drive away, whether they were taken in or not. The workhouse accepted them reluctantly.

By the end of the Famine, in 1850, 119,628 children under fifteen years old remained in the workhouses, at a cost to the state of one shilling a week each. Forty per cent of them had been orphaned or deserted.

CHAPTER 7

1847

Fever

Previous famines in Ireland had been accompanied by fever, and this famine was no exception. Typhus fever (transmitted by lice, a fact which was not confirmed for another sixty years) affected the blood circulation, making the patient's face swell up and darken, and was called 'black fever'. The symptoms included raging temperature and delirium, with a rash, vomiting and occasionally gangrene. One of the worst features of the fever was the smell, 'an almost intolerable stench'.

Relapsing fever, causing vomiting, was also carried by lice. The patient would relapse six days or so after the first onset, and this could be repeated three or four times. It was often accompanied by jaundice, and so was called 'yellow fever' in Irish.

Conditions were perfect for the spread of these diseases. Clothing had been sold for food, so the poorest wore only filthy, lice-infested rags. They had been severely weakened

I regret to announce the death of Catherine McEvoy, the widow of P. McEvoy, from actual want. I have since received the depositions taken by the coroner, which I now forward. It appears that the screams of the unfortunate woman were heard at a very considerable distance, and no-one would go near her until death put an end to her sufferings ... The Guardian ... has sent this poor woman's only child to the workhouse at Cavan.

by starvation, and in the extremely cold winter of 1846-47 they gathered together to keep warm. Because of the wet weather, and because people had had no energy to cut turf during the summer months, there was a shortage of fuel.

The Irish custom of hospitality meant that shelter was never refused to a stranger, and fever was often passed on in this way. The crowds of people on the public works also made it easy for the lice to spread, and one infected person could infect a hundred more in one day.

Other illnesses spreading at this time included bacillary dysentery, or the 'bloody flux'. Infected bacilli multiply in the bowels, causing ulcers, gangrene and diarrhoea, with agonizing pain. 'It was easily known if any of the inmates in the cabins of the poor were suffering from this disease, as the ground in such places was marked with clots of blood.' Though not infectious, 'famine dropsy' was also widespread, causing swelling of the body and limbs. This is now known as hunger oedema, caused by the last stages of starvation.

Ordinary dysentery was common, killing children rather than adults. The eye infection, ophthalmia, spread rapidly in the overcrowded workhouse conditions, and hundreds of children lost their sight, partially or totally. Scurvy, causing teeth to drop out and joints to swell, had been almost unknown in pre-Famine Ireland, because it is caused by lack of Vitamin C, which is plentiful in potatoes. Now it affected thousands of people, often causing fatal haemorrhaging.

Above: Funeral at Shepperton Lakes, near Skibbereen, Co Cork, early 1847

Below: Funeral procession of Daniel O'Connell in Dublin, 5 Aug 1847

Go where you might, every object reminded you of the fearful desolation that was progressing around you. The features of the people were gaunt, their eyes wild and hollow, and their gait feeble and tottering. Pass through the fields, and you were met by little groups bearing home on their shoulders, and that with difficulty, a coffin, or perhaps two of them. The roads were literally black with funerals; and as you passed along from parish to parish, the death-bells were pealing forth, in slow but dismal tones, the gloomy triumph which pestilence was achieving over the face of our devoted country ... Under the terrible pressure of the complex destitution which prevailed, everything like shame was forgotten, and it was well known that whole families, who had hitherto been respectable and independent, were precipitated, almost at once, into all the common cant of importunity and clamour during this frightful struggle between life and death. Of the truth of this, the scenes which took place at the public soup shops, and other appointed places of relief, afforded melancholy proof. Here were wild crowds, ragged, sickly, and wasted away to skin and bone, struggling for the dole of charity like so many hungry vultures about the remnants of some carcase which they were tearing, amid noises, and screams, and strife, into very shreds; for, as we have said, all sense of becoming restraint or shame was now abandoned, and the timid girl, or modest mother of a family, or decent farmer, goaded by the same wild and tyrannical solicitation and outcry as if they had been trained since their very infancy to all the forms of impudent cant and imposture ...

The dreadful typhus was now abroad in all its deadly power, accompanied, on this occasion, as it always is among the Irish, by a panic, which invested it with tenfold terrors. The moment fever was ascertained, or even supposed, to visit a family, that moment the infected persons were avoided by their neighbours and friends as if they carried death, as they often did, about them, so that its presence occasioned all the usual interchanges of civility and good-neighbourhood to be discontinued ....

Hospital Care

In 1846 a Central Board of Health had been set up, to run hospitals and dispensaries, but it was soon closed down, because there was very little sickness or fever to treat at that time, only starvation. As typhus began to spread, there were only 28 hospitals in Ireland, and none at all in the more remote areas. Frenchpark, County Roscommon, with a population of 30,000 spread over 135 miles, had only one hospital.

There were about 500 out-patient dispensaries, but again these were few and far between. Even so, more money had been spent on hospitals in Ireland than in Britain, and every county had an infirmary. Medical care was mainly preventive — infected clothes were baked to kill the fever, and infected areas were fumigated with sulphuric acid.

Reports of fever began to come in to the Relief Commissioners in early 1847; people were dying quickly, in frightful numbers, and typhus was spreading like wildfire. The Central Board of Health was reappointed until August 1850, and by the end of its life it had opened 373 temporary fever hospitals.

The workhouse hospitals were far too small to deal with the numbers pouring in. Almost every inmate was now suffering with some form of illness, but there was no space to keep the sick away from those who were well. Temporary wooden fever wards, called 'fever sheds', were erected in some places, but many workhouses did not have the money to do this. Medical care became more and more difficult. The doctor in Enniskillen workhouse had to give up vaccinating for smallpox, 'from the reduced condition of the children from want of food and sufficient diet, as the incision made in the arm to receive the infection becomes a sloughing gangrene, which produces almost certain death'.

The government finally accepted the fact of an epidemic, and brought in an Irish Fever Act in April 1847. This put the responsibility for health care on the relief committees, instead of on the overburdened and debt-ridden Boards of Guardians. The relief committees could overrule the Guardians and do whatever was necessary for fever patients, without having to obey the Poor Law rules. The costs would be met by the government. The Act was successful in most of its aims, and the final cost was £119,055.

The numbers who died of fever, probably ten times more than those who died of hunger, will never be known. Thousands simply disappeared, never reaching the hospitals or workhouses. Where bodies were buried at all, it was rarely in churchyards any more, but in unmarked hillside graves. There was no legal register for deaths, and relief committees found it impossible to estimate the numbers.

Typhus fever affected those in authority very badly, the middle-aged middle classes. Because of the strain it put on the heart, older people were very vulnerable to it. Where forms of fever had always been endemic, many of the poor had formed an immunity to it during their youth, but doctors and medical officers, priests and clergymen, relieving officers and workhouse officials all took the fever, and many died. Seven doctors died in County Cavan in 1847, and forty-eight in the province of Munster. Of 473 medical officers appointed by the Board of Health, one out of every thirteen died.

There was a high death rate among priests and clergymen as well. They were already exhausted from shortage of food, and from endless work on relief committees, writing letters and petitions and doing everything they could to help their people. Now the Catholic priests, determined to give the Sacrament of the Dying wherever they could, were at great risk of catching the fever at every deathbed they attended.

In the diocese of Killaloe, for example, six priests died between 1846 and 1847.

Meanwhile, Church of Ireland clergy assisted the Society of Friends in distributing aid, and running soup kitchens. In 1847, forty Protestant clergy died of fever. Unfortunately, however, Catholic and Protestant clergy chose in general not to come together on relief work, and this probably meant that some efforts were not as efficient as they could have been.

Famine scene in Old Chapel Lane, Skibbereen, Co Cork, from the Illustrated London News, *13 February 1847*

Killooly Hall,
Frankford, November 24th, 1847.

SIR,

I beg to send you a copy of resolutions passed *unanimously* at a meeting of the Landed Proprietors, Householders, and Occupiers of the Electoral Division of Killoughy, held this day at Mountbolus—Major BARRY FOX in the chair—and request an answer at your earliest convenience.

I have the honor to be, SIR,

Your Obedient Servant,

R. W. GAMBLE, Secretary.

~~~~~~

Resolved,—

1st,—That we deeply lament the awful state of destitution at present existing in this Division ; that we acknowledge the justice, the humanity, and the absolute necessity of every really destitute person being fully relieved ; that we clearly perceive that the expenditure necessary for that relief, if given without any return in the way of labour or otherwise, must (in addition to its degrading moral influence,) inevitably ruin most of the small holders, and press exceedingly heavy upon all classes, however circumstanced. Yet however great that destitution, and however inadequate the property of the Division to meet it, we cannot in justice seek for assistance elsewhere until we have ourselves made use of our utmost exertions for its alleviation ; and we hereby resolve that we will endeavour, by every means in our power, to provide employment for the destitute, as the only salutary mode of relief.

2nd,—That we, the Landed Proprietors of this Division, will keep in employment for four months previous to April next, one man for every £25 value, according to the Poor Law valuation of our estates in said Division, over and above the number of men usually employed by us, or that we will agree with and allow our tenants for employing same on *our* behalf.

3rd,—That we, the Householders and Occupiers of said Division, whose holdings are valued over £25 per annum under the Poor Law, will keep in employment for four months, previous to the 1st of April next, one man for every £25 of said value over and above our usual number of men.

4th,—That as the *Resident* Proprietors of this Division represent only one-third of the property within it, we earnestly request the co-operation of those *Non-Resident*, which if we fail to obtain, it must in a great degree paralyze every effort of the former ; and that this meeting be now adjourned to the 1st of December next, in order to obtain their reply as to whether they will join with their Tenants and the other Proprietors in the foregoing plan for the employment of the destitute.

RICHARD W. GAMBLE, Secretary.

This circular was issued by Richard W. Gamble, Secretary of Killoughy Relief Committee, King's County (now Co Offaly) It lists the resolutions passed by a meeting of landed proprietors, householders and occupiers on 24 November 1847. Resident proprietors agreed to offer employment in proportion to the amount of property which they held. However, they appealed to absentee proprietors, who held two thirds of the property in the district, for help.

In the Cities

In March 1847, a ship carrying fever-ridden emigrants was forced by bad weather to put into Belfast, and typhus fever swept through the city. Hordes of famine victims were pouring into Belfast, seeking relief, and the epidemic reached its peak in July. 'Hundreds,' said the *Belfast Newsletter*, 'are daily exposed in the delirium of this frightful malady, on the streets, or left to die in their filthy and ill-ventilated hovels... It is now a thing of daily occurrence to see haggard, sallow and emaciated beings, stricken down by fever or debility from actual want, stretched prostrate upon the footways of our streets and bridges.' A Board of Health was set up, a temporary hospital was constructed, and the workhouse infirmary was enlarged.

The mortality was particularly heavy in cities, because of the intense overcrowding and dirt of the slums. The fever epidemic in Dublin reached its worst in June, and did not begin to decline until February 1848. One thousand more beds were provided than in any earlier epidemic, bringing the number to 2,500, but up to 12,000 famine victims applied to Cork Street Hospital in ten months. 'It was quite common to find three, four or even five ill in a house when application had been made only for one.'

Dr Callanan wrote of Cork city: 'From the commencement of 1847...Fate opened her book in good earnest here, and the full tide of death flowed on everywhere around us. During the first six months of that dark period *one-third* of the daily population of our streets consisted of shadows and spectres, the impersonations of disease and famine, crowding in from the rural districts, and stalking along to the general doom — the grave — which appeared to await them at the distance of a few steps or a few short hours.' Householders and shopkeepers frequently found the bodies of victims propped against their doors in the morning, where they had tried to shelter overnight.

Control of Infection

It was some time before it was realised that typhus fever was infectious. Ballinrobe workhouse, County Mayo, admitted a strolling beggar in February 1847, and some days later he died of typhus. Large numbers followed him as the fever swept through the workhouse, helped by the overcrowded conditions. Of the staff, the doctor, chaplain, master, matron and clerk all became infected, and only two survived. Ninety-five people died in Lurgan workhouse (County Antrim) in one week, but fifty-two of them had been healthy when they arrived, and had caught it from the inmates already there.

People began to learn about infection, and the age-old hospitality of the Irish disappeared almost overnight. Strangers were avoided, and if even one member of a family became infected, the whole family was left alone. Fever was often caught through contact with the dead; after death, the lice would leave the cooling body and transfer themselves to anyone nearby. People became afraid to bury the dead, and often pulled down cabins and burned them over the corpses inside instead.

It was impossible to increase the size of burial-grounds, because the living were afraid of having those who died of fever buried near them. Workhouse yards became burial grounds, and bodies were buried in huge pits, in batches. The huge number of bodies needing burial, and the lack of resources, led to the use of 'hinged coffins' or 'sliding coffins'. When the bottom of the coffin was opened, the corpse would slide into the mass grave and the coffin could be used again. Each body was covered with clay and lime, and some pits held up to fifty bodies.

Ravages of Fever

Dr Stephens was sent to report on the workhouse in Bantry, County Cork. 'As I entered the house the stench that proceeded from it was most dreadful and noisome; but, oh! what scenes presented themselves to my view as I proceeded through the wards and passages: patients lying on straw, naked and in their excrements, a light covering over them — in two beds living beings beside the dead, in the same bed with them and dead since the night before. There was no medicine — no drink — no fire...'

Canon O'Rourke, writing in 1870, gave an impressionistic account of the ravages of disease: 'Some idea of the dreadful mortality then prevalent in Cork may be found from the fact that in one day thirty-six bodies were interred in the same grave; the deaths in the workhouse there from 27 December 1846, until the middle of April — less than four months —

The Famine Year (The Stricken Land)
by Lady Wilde

'Weary men, what reap ye? Golden corn for the stranger.
What sow ye? Human corpses that wait for the avenger.
Fainting forms, hunger-stricken, what see you in the offing?
Stately ships to bear our food away, amid the stranger's scoffing.
There's a proud array of soldiers — what do they round your door?
They guard our master's granaries from the thin hands of the poor.
Pale mothers, wherefore weeping?
Would to God that we were dead;
Our children swoon before us, and we cannot give them bread.'

amounted to 2,130... On 16 April there were upwards of 300 cases of fever in the Carrick-on-Shannon workhouse and the weekly deaths amounted to fifty. Again: every avenue leading to the plague-stricken town of Macroom had a fever hospital; persons of all ages were dropping dead in the streets.

'In May it was announced that fever continued to rage with unabated fury at Castlebar. "Sligo is a plague spot; disease in every street, and of the worst kind." "Fever is committing fearful ravages in Ballindine, Ballinrobe, Claremorris, Westport, Ballina and Belmullet, all in the county of Mayo." From Roscommon, the news came that the increase of fever was truly awful; the hospitals were full and applicants were daily refused admission. "No one can tell," said the writer, "what becomes of these unfortunate beings; they are brought away by their pauper friends, and no more is heard of them."'

CHAPTER 8

1847-48

Evictions

As the costs of the famine and the Poor Law began to weigh more and more heavily on Irish landlords, the scene was set for the clearances, or evictions, which complete the picture of misery of these years.

As each landlord was responsible for paying the rates of every tenant who paid less than £4 in yearly rent, those whose land was crowded with poor tenants were now facing huge bills. They couldn't collect rent, let alone rates, from the wretches on their estates. The only way to collect enough money was to clear the poor from their small plots, and to relet the land in bigger lots, to people with more money.

It is unknown how many were evicted before 1848, when the police began to keep records of evictions, but between 1849 and 1854, 49,000 families were dispossessed. As the rate collectors pressed harder and harder, more and more tenants were evicted by desperate landlords.

But the landlords felt justified; they were facing large

debts themselves. The Marquis of Sligo owed £1,650 to Westport Union, in 1848; he could only pay it by borrowing, and his debts and mortgages already came to £6,000 per year. But Captain Arthur Kennedy, a Poor Law inspector in Kilrush, County Clare, later said: '...there were days in that western county when I came back from some scene of eviction so maddened by the sights of hunger and misery I had seen in the day's work that I felt disposed to take the gun from behind my door and shoot the first landlord I met.'

There had been some clearances in 1846, but the great wave of evictions came in 1847. There were also thousands of 'voluntary' surrenders, where tenants simply surrendered possession of their patch of land and began to beg, usually heading for the nearest town. Of course these were just as much evictions as the official ones — there was precious little 'voluntary' about them. In other cases tenants were persuaded to accept a small sum of money, and sometimes they helped to tear down their poor dwellings themselves. They were cheated into believing the workhouse would take them in.

One of the worst areas for evictions was West Clare, as landlords turned thousands of families onto the road and demolished their inadequate cabins. In April 1848, Captain Kennedy calculated that 1,000 houses had been levelled since November, with an average of six people to each house. In Birr, County Offaly, a man called Denis Duffy was evicted, although he was ill: 'Duffy was brought out and laid under a shed, covered with turf, which was once used as a pig cabin, and his house thrown down. The landlord, not deeming the possession to be complete while the pig cabin remained entire, ordered the roof to be removed, and poor Duffy, having no friend to shelter him, remained under the open air for two days and two nights, until death put an end to his sufferings'.

The evicted families would shelter in ditches, until bad

No.	DENOMINATIONS.	TENANTS.	Rent, when due.	Arrears.	Half-Year's Rent.	Half Year's Rent Charge, in lieu of tithe, due 1 May 1849.
		Forward £	5928 4 4	7630 7 1	441 7 4	
367 365	Que et Ballinaboilagh	Duggan Patrick		18 0 0	6 0 0	
368 366	"	p Duggan John		12 0 0	6 0 0	.. ..
369 367	.	p Lynch Thomas		36 0 0	18 0 0	
370 368	.	p Lynch James		44 0 0	11 0 0	
371 369	.	p Scearle Timothy up.		23 0 0	3 17 0	
372 370	.	p Corcoran John		24 0 0	8 0 0	
373 371	.	p Fohy Denis		28 16 11	9 0 0	
374 372	.	p Fohy Mary		40 0 0	9 0 0	
375 373	.	p Mahony John		41 16 0	7 12 0	
376 374	.	p Mahony Denis		21 0 0	21 0 0	
377 375	.	p Frahy John		30 0 0	10 0 0	
378 376	.	p Murray Martin Denis		31 0 0	13 0 0	
379 377	.	p Murphy Martin		32 0 0	8 0 0	
380 378	.	p Murphy Martin		4 15 0	4 15 0	
381 379	.	p -any James		39 0 0	13 0 0	
382 380	.	p Cronin Michael		27 12 0	0 12 0	
383 381	.	p Murphy John Martin		44 0 0	8 0 0	
384 3	.	p Murphy Edward		26 0 0	8 16 0	
385 383	.	p Murphy Martin Mick		20 10 0	10 0 0	
386 384	.	p Murphy John Mick		41 12 0	10 0 0	

Left: Ejectment of Irish tenantry, Illustrated London News, 16 December 1848
Above: extract from rental of the Earl of Midleton's estate in counties Cork and Waterford,
7 August 1847. Transcript of the right hand column appears below.

No 368	Received notice to quit
No 369	Two of the tenants, Jeremiah and John Hegarty sent to Canada, their portion of arrear will be lost.
No 370	Tenant dead notice to quit given to his widow
No 372	Tenant removed arrear lost
No 373	Arrear lost tenant sent to Canada
No 375, 376 and 377	Notices to quit at March next given
No 379	Arrear lost tenant sent to Canada
No 380	Received notice to quit at March next
No 381	Arrear lost tenant sent to Canada
No 382 & 384	Notices to quit at March next given in these two numbers
No 386	To be removed by ejectment
No 387	Arrear lost tenant sent to Canada
No 390 & 391	Notices given to quit at March next

These helpless creatures are not only unhoused, but often driven off the land, no one remaining on the lands being allowed to lodge or harbour them. Or they, perhaps, linger about the spot, and frame some temporary shelter out of the materials of their old homes against a broken wall, or behind a ditch or fence, or in a bog-hole (scalps as they are called), places totally unfit for human habitations; or they crowd into some of the few neighbouring cabins still left standing, when allowed to do so, as lodgers, where such numbers usually congregate that disease, together with the privations of other kinds which they endure, before long carry them off. As soon as one horde of houseless and all but naked paupers are dead, or provided for in the workhouse, another wholesale eviction doubles the number, who in their turn pass through the same ordeal of wandering from house to house, or burrowing in bogs or behind ditches, till broken down by privation and exposure to the elements, they seek the workhouse, or die by the roadside.

weather drove them to seek the workhouse. These were people to whom ten miles away was 'foreign', who might never have travelled from their home place all their lives.

Next to Clare, the worst area for evictions was County Mayo, the scene of ten per cent of all evictions between 1849 and 1854. Among the worst landlords was the Earl of Lucan, who owned over 60,000 acres, and had once said that 'he would not breed paupers to pay priests'. He removed over 2,000 tenants in the parish of Ballinrobe alone, and restocked the cleared land as grazing farms. The Marquis of Sligo was also an evicting landlord, but he claimed to be selective, only getting rid of the idle and dishonest. He cleared about one-quarter of his tenants altogether.

Some of the evictions might have taken place earlier if it had not been for fear of the threats of the secret societies, but these were now greatly weakened by the Famine. However, revenge was still occasionally taken, and seven landlords were shot, six fatally, during the autumn and winter of 1847.

Ten other occupiers of land, though without tenants, were also murdered. Lord Clarendon was alarmed that this meant rebellion, and he asked for special powers to combat crime.

Lord John Russell was not sympathetic to this appeal, believing that the landlords themselves were largely responsible for the tragedy in the first place. He remarked, '...It is quite true that landlords in England would not like to be shot like hares and partridges...but neither does any landlord in England turn out fifty persons at once and burn their houses over their heads, giving them no provision for the future.' However, a compromise was reached, and a Crime and Outrage Act was passed in December, 1847. Extra troops were sent to Ireland, and regulations about carrying arms were tightened.

Emigration

Not all the landlords who evicted tenants threw them on the side of the road. Emigration from Ireland had been common for some time, and there now began some 'assisted emigration', whereby landlords gave their tenants enough money for a passage to America or Canada. Some landlords even hired ships to transport them. One-quarter of a million people left Ireland in 1847 (about 5,000 of them landlord-assisted) and 200,000 or more every year for the next five years.

Only three or four per cent of emigrants overall were helped by landlords, but others got aid from charities, or had been sent money by family members who had gone already.

By the time this massive shift of population had begun to die down, almost two million people had left the small island of Ireland forever. At first, the landlords who helped people to go were praised for their efforts, but by 1848 there was a

change of tone. Priests, politicians and newspapers began to attack this enforced exile, accusing Britain of trying to annihilate the population.

Between 1815 and the start of the Famine, almost 1.5 million Irish people had already left Ireland, mainly going to England, the United States, Canada and Australia. The difference between this earlier emigration and the Famine-driven flood was that those who had left by choice, seeking a better life, were mainly the young and strong, 70 per cent of them aged between 16 and 34.

By contrast, the millions who fled from the Famine contained large numbers of the very old and the very young, and were often weakened by fever and want before they even started. In those days, the journey to such countries as the United States was exhausting and full of hardship, even if the conditions were good, and you had to be fit for it.

The earlier emigrations, after 1815, had been caused by poor economic conditions after the Napoleonic War, and had been encouraged by cheap sailings. There was a large amount of trade between America and Britain, but the ships returning to America were often almost empty. Emigrants were a profitable way to fill these ships. Better routes to Canada were being opened up as well, and English

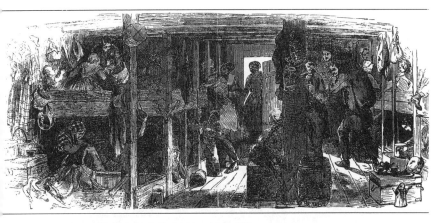

Dormitory life between decks on the emigrant ship.

Facing page: The Ocean Monarch, an emigrant ship which caught fire and sank off Liverpool on 24 August 1848. It had just set sail for America with 306 people on board. 178 were lost in the shipwreck. Illustrated London News, 2 September 1848. The Ocean Monarch was one of 59 emigrant ships to America which sank in the years 1847-53.

Kilcock, Co Kildare, threatening note sent to James Flanagan on 6 January 1848

Sir — We the people of the district that you collected the Poor Rates in, in either Boush or Innismacthesant, or any other part that you collect the Poor Rate in, or take up any distress, or drives any person's cattle for the Rates, we will be under the necessity of shooting you in the open daylight, for we may as well loose our lives as to loose our support; so if you don't like this warning we give you, take your own advice, for we are determined to stop you or any other person that will come to collect them till the times mend.

James Flanagan,
There is your doom,
so if like it
continue.

The Government Medical Inspector's Office at Liverpool, Illustrated London News, 6 July 1850

shipowners began to get in on the traffic. By 1831, you could go from Newry (County Down) to Liverpool and then to New York for only three pounds.

This was still a large sum of money, so many emigrants just went as far as Britain. The largest proportion of these early emigrants were of Scots Presbyterian stock, from Ulster, because the linen industry there was declining. The English Poor Law provided Outdoor Relief more freely than in Ireland, and the food was better. Steam passenger ferries began to cross the Irish Sea during the 1820s, and the competition among ports and among ferry companies kept prices low. The ferries were often overcrowded, as passengers made a last-minute rush to get on board. The shipping companies delayed proper regulation as long as they could, because it would cut profits.

Between 1846 and 1852, over one million people left Ireland. Emigration continued to drain the country, once the pattern had been established. It is estimated that four million left between 1851 and 1910, and at least one-fifth of this

---

LETTER FROM AN IRISH EMIGRANT TO LORD MONTEAGLE.

Melbourne, Port Philip,
20th of March, 1848.

My Lord,

I, as in duty bound, feel called upon to inform your Lordship how the Emigrants who obtained a passage through your lordship's intercession are situated. All the Girls are employed in the Town of Melbourne, at the rate of Twenty-five to Twenty-six pounds per annum; they are all in respectable places. Thos. Sheahan is employed in the Town adjoining, attending Bricklayers at Four Shillings and Six pence per day—John Enraght on Public work, at the same rate. The general hire for Labourers of every description, my lord, is from Twenty-eight to Thirty-two pounds per annum, with board and lodgings. There is nothing in such demand in this Colony as Male and Female Servants: I was employed myself, my lord, on board the Lady Peel, by the Colonial Doctor, filling up forms of agreement between Masters and Servants, so that I had an opportunity of knowing all the particulars concerning wages, term of employment, occupation, &c. &c.

I would mention all, but I consider your lordship will feel satisfied when you know they are all in good situations, and with respectable masters and mistresses. I have seen a good deal of the Emigrants whom I knew at home, that obtained a passage through your lordship's intercession, about eleven years ago, some of them live in the Town of Melbourne, and are living comfortably. Ellen Shanahan (Loughill), is married to one Rockford, in this Town, and keeps a Hotel. Maurice Connors, of Foynes, is living in this Town, and has as much money spared as exempts him from personal labour. I have heard from some more of them who live in the Country, and as far as I can learn, my lord, they are living independently. Ellen Sheahan is just going up to her brother accompanied by her first cousin, Daniel Mulcare, of Clounlikard, himself and his brother has lived some time in this Town, and kept a Grocer's Shop. They have acted the part of a brother to me, my lord, they gave me the best of entertainment, and procured a situation for me with one Mr. Ham, a Surveyor. I am going up the Country to the Avoca River to survey a Station; my wages are Twenty-one pounds for six months. Mr. Hurley has sent for his nephew and his aunt, they are on their way up by this time. I expect, my lord, to be able to remit some money to your lordship in recompense for the expenses incurred on my and my sisters' account by your lordship, as well as some relief to my poor mother, brothers and sister. I hope, my lord, this humble but imperfect epistle will find your Lordship, Lady Monteagle, Mr. Spring Rice, and all his family in good health. Any information I can give your lordship respecting the interior of this Country, will not be lost sight of on my part. Mr. Thos. Ham, of Great Collins Street, Melbourne, would forward any commands to me, my lord, if your lordship should want any more information concerning any of the late or former Emigrants. Every thing in this Colony, my lord, is from three to four times as dear here as it is in England or Ireland, except Bread, Beef, Mutton, &c., the best of which is obtained at Three half-pence to Two-pence per lb.

I am, My Lord, with profound veneration,
Your Lordship's most devoted Servant,
P. DANAHER,

P.S. My Sisters also, my lord, beg leave to return their most sincere thanks to your Lordship and Lady Monteagle.

John Flanagan and Wife are both employed by a man of the name of Murphy, a Brewer, about twelve miles out in the Country, wages Fifty pounds per annum.

Letter sent to Lord Monteagle by a tenant whose passage to Australia he had paid, telling how well he and other emigrants from Shanagolden were faring. This letter was printed in circular form to encourage emigration.

emigration was to Britain. Thousands flooded into Liverpool, creating huge problems of overcrowding and disease, and three-quarters of those who sailed across the Atlantic left from this port. The size of the remittances sent back home was notable; between 1848 and 1870, over sixteen million pounds arrived in Ireland from the USA.

Hazards of Emigration

Because so many people had already emigrated over the previous decades, emigration was seen as a common-sense response to the appalling conditions at home. In most European countries, emigration was the last resort in bad economic conditions, but in Ireland emigration began in a matter of months after the first crop failure. Newspapers carried advertisements, placards were pasted up everywhere — the passenger companies were determined to encourage large numbers to travel.

One of the strongest 'pull' factors was the stream of letters home, praising the new life and urging family members to follow. Of course, emigrants who had not done well in their new homes soon lost touch with their families out of shame, so the letters that did arrive may have given a slightly unrealistic picture of the fine prospects. Once the Famine had tightened its grip, it was not just the poor who emigrated. Merchants and tradesmen, watching the economy collapse, were being crippled by heavy taxation. Large numbers of the entrepreneurial class began to leave as well.

Until 1850, when iron-hulled screw steamers were introduced, it took at least a month to cross the Atlantic. Travellers were given a basic minimum of food and water, but had to provide anything else themselves. The packed holds were a fertile ground for typhus. Only a very small number of these vessels were wrecked, but the wrecks were widely reported and vividly described, adding to the fears of the trip.

The worst death rate among emigrants occurred in 1847, when the notorious 'coffin ships' travelled to Canada; of over 100,000 emigrants making this trip, one-sixth died on board ship or soon after landing. Possibly about 5 per cent of the Famine emigrants died; the normal death rate, however, was about 2 per cent.

Ships' officers described the appalling conditions: '...friendless emigrants stowed away like bales of cotton, and packed like slaves in a slave ship; confined in a place that, during storm time, must be closed against both light and air, who can do no cooking, nor warm so much as a cup of water... Passengers are cut off from the most indispensable conveniences of a civilised dwelling... We had not been at sea one week, when to hold your head down the fore-hatchway was like holding it down a suddenly opened cess pool'.

Despite all the reasons to be afraid of the journey, nothing could stop desperate people determined to go. They would have to face seasickness, insanitary accommodation, violent fellow passengers and often the hostility of the crew, as well as rotten food and foul water, and they would have to fight off the crooks and touts who tried to rob and cheat them both before and after the journey. 'Trappers' or confidence tricksters hung around the ports in Ireland and Liverpool to rob the unwary and illiterate travellers, and 'runners' waited at the other end, to entice them into 'boarding-houses' which were no more than robbers' dens.

An example of the notorious 'coffin ships' was the barque *Elizabeth and Sarah*, which sailed from County Mayo in July 1846, heading for Canada. She carried 276 persons, instead of the 212 listed, and had only 8,700 gallons of water for the

Above: Overcrowded emigrant ship leaving Ireland

William Steuart Trench

I shall not readily forget the scenes that occurred in Kenmare when I returned, and announced that I was prepared at Lord Lansdowne's expense to send to America every one now in the poor-house who was chargeable to his lordship's estate, and who desired to go; leaving each to select what port in America he pleased — whether Boston, New York, New Orleans or Quebec.

The announcement at first was scarcely credited; it was considered by the paupers to be too good news to be true. But when it began to be believed and appreciated, a rush was made to get away at once.

Two hundred each week were selected of those apparently most suited for emigration: and having arranged their slender outfit, a steady man, on whom I could depend, Mr. Jeremiah O'Shea, was employed to take charge of them on their journey to Cork, and not to leave them nor allow them to scatter, until he saw them safely on board the emigrant ship.

voyage, instead of the 12,532 gallons she should have had. Each passenger was entitled to be given 7 lbs of provisions each week, but none was ever distributed. The 276 passengers shared 32 berths, and there was no sanitary facility of any kind. The voyage took eight weeks, because the captain took the wrong course, and by the time the ship broke down and was towed into the St Lawrence river in September, 42 people had died.

By this time the authorities in Canada and the United States thought they knew what to expect from the emigrant ships — thousands of emigrants had arrived already, and their numbers and poverty had caused the passing of various Passenger Acts, forbidding emigrants who had no money or subsistence to land. But no-one expected the 'ship fever' of 1847, that is, the typhus fever which now crossed the Atlantic as well.

In 1847, the St Lawrence river, the entrance route to Canada, stayed frozen over until May, much later than usual. The first ship which then arrived at Grosse Ile, the quarantine station, had 84 cases of fever on board (nine had died). They had all come from Ireland, via Britain. The quarantine hospital could only accommodate 200 people, but eight more ships arrived carrying 430 fever cases, and three days later seventeen more ships. By May 26, thirty vessels waited at Grosse Ile to be cleared, with 10,000 emigrants on board. By May 31 this had risen to forty ships, stretching two miles down the river.

Conditions became intolerable. Tents were hastily erected on land, but patients were often left for days on the ships without treatment. Most of the ships had not one healthy person on board, and those who had escaped fever were weakened by starvation. Processions of boats carried the sick and dead from the ships, flinging them on the beach to crawl to the hospital if they could.

By the middle of the summer, it was impossible to

quarantine people properly, and they were allowed to stay on the ships for fifteen days, instead of spending ten days in the hospital. This meant the sick and healthy were still cooped up together, and fever spread as before. By the end of July, quarantine efforts had been abandoned, and the hordes of emigrants were just sent on inland. The result was that Quebec and Montreal later suffered widespread fever epidemics.

After 1848, stricter controls were enforced, and the emigrant death rates fell dramatically. A monument on Grosse Ile, at the site of the emigrant cemetery, bears the inscription, 'In this secluded spot lie the mortal remains of 5,294 persons, who, flying from pestilence and famine in Ireland in the year 1847, found in America but a grave.'

The United States had responded with great generosity to the appeals from famine-stricken Ireland, and thousands of dollars in aid had been sent, as well as food supplies and clothing. However, the American authorities were appalled at the sudden influx of starving, impoverished emigrants, too ill and weak to work, and were more successful than the Canadians at enforcing the Passenger Acts. Ships which arrived with destitute passengers were forbidden to land them, and were turned back to sea, to the despair of those on board. Many of these ships then headed to Canada instead.

The Irish were not welcome emigrants. Apart from their poverty and the fever they often carried, they had no suitable skills or trades, and most of them were so weakened they were unfit for work of any kind, even the unskilled agricultural labour they had been used to. They tended to drift to the slums of the large cities, supporting themselves by unskilled labour. Often they drank, to cover the despair and loneliness of unsuccessful emigration, and fighting was frequent. Child mortality was huge; in Boston, 61 percent of children died under the age of five between 1841 and 1845, even before the new wave of emigrants began to arrive.

The Irish tended to congregate in 'Irish quarters', and they stayed in the cities — only about ten per cent moved on to rural areas. They were fodder for the political bosses, and became notorious for drunken rows and violent crime. It took a long time for the Famine emigrants to overcome their disadvantages, and to begin to make a positive contribution to the countries they had reached.

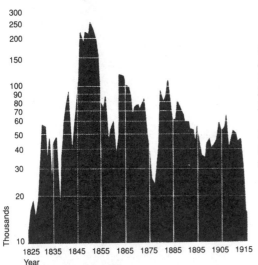

Chart showing Irish overseas emigration, 1825-1915. Numbers leaving the United Kingdom per annum.

Below: Cork Harbour, the point of departure for many.

Above: Emigrants at Cork: a scene on the quay
Below: Accommodation was often a cramped space between decks, Illustrated London News, July 1850

CHAPTER 9

1848–49

Crop fails again

The potato crop of 1847 was not affected by blight, because weather conditions were too dry, but the crop itself, though sound, was far too small to make any difference to the ongoing tragedy. Enormous efforts were therefore made to increase the 1848 crop, and farmers strained to plant as

Sligo Union 19 February 1848

A boy of 14, named James Foley ... left the Killanummery hospital on 22nd January, being a week convalescent after fever; he received from the doctor who had been in charge of the hospital, which was at that time ordered to be closed, a ticket of admission to the hospital at Manorhamilton; the boy, instead of going there, returned to his father, who, fearing contagion, would not admit him among his other children, and probably from want of shelter, in addition to his weak state of health, the poor boy perished in the inclement weather, or it might have been from a relapse. The father was in the receipt of out-door relief for himself and his children, including the boy James, and he did not report either his being in hospital, or his subsequent condition to the relieving officer.

many potatoes as possible.

The total acreage of potatoes in 1848 was three times more
than that in 1847, but that summer was extremely wet. The
blight raged again, and the crop was lost. The Quakers were
asked to re-establish soup kitchens, but refused. Their
workers were physically exhausted and their resources had
almost run out. Besides, they felt that free alms were
damaging to the people in the long run.

Young Ireland rebellion

During all this time of increasing hopelessness and despair,
one group of men was still actively working towards
revolution, believing that the only answer was for Ireland to
be in a position of independence. These were the Young
Irelanders, who had broken from Daniel O'Connell's Repeal
Movement in 1846 because they were not convinced by his
doctrine of 'moral force', and wanted radical solutions to
Ireland's problems.

A mood of revolution was sweeping over Europe in 1848,
with rebellions in Austria and Italy. In France, the monarchy
was overthrown and a republic was proclaimed (again). The
British government was growing increasingly nervous of the
Chartists, a working-class movement seeking civil rights.

The Young Irelanders began to form 'revolutionary clubs' all over Ireland, seeking the overthrow of the state.

This movement for change coincided with a new tenant rights movement, spearheaded by James Fintan Lalor and supported by John Mitchel, son of a Presbyterian, and a spellbinding orator. Lalor held that the land should belong to the community as a whole, and that tenants were entitled to secure tenure and fixed rents. He hoped to achieve this change peacefully, through a national rent strike. However, this movement was before its time; the people were too broken by misfortune to care, and the landlords were vehemently opposed to tenant right. Mitchel began to consider violent revolution as the only means of change, and founded a firebrand newspaper called the *United Irishman* in January 1848.

The government, galvanised by the threat of rebellion, sent 10,000 troops into Ireland. Leaders of the movement, including Mitchel, William Smith O'Brien and Thomas

'The Union!' by Thomas Rowlandson, 1801

The factory (one of the auxiliary houses) with 200 inmates, is left in charge of a pauper; Ballyerra (another auxiliary house) with 126 sick children, is also left in charge of paupers and there is no paid officer at Broomhill (another house). There are over 1500 children, with only one male and one female teacher; and the duties of assistant matron at Leadmore are also imposed on the schoolmistress. She has been for some weeks in fever, and her double duty is performed by her sister.

Francis Meagher ('Meagher of the Sword') were arrested and charged with sedition, but were released on bail. O'Brien and Meagher went to Paris, seeking aid, but had no success — the new French government did not want to antagonise Britain. Meanwhile the Catholic Church was working against them through the parish priests, who were very influential. Pope Pius IX forbade priests to engage in political activities, and suspended Father Kenyon, in Tipperary, who had pledged himself to Young Ireland.

In May 1848 O'Brien and Meagher were tried, but the prosecutions failed and they were freed. However, when Mitchel came to trial, the jury was 'packed', and troops filled the street outside. He was found guilty, and sentenced to transportation to Australia for fourteen years, with hard labour in the penal colonies. After the trial, his comrades began to plan a rebellion, collecting money and arms.

It seems extraordinary that they could have expected such a project to succeed. Destitution was worse than ever, and beggars were pouring into every town. Jail had become a place of safety, because at least food was available there, and people were so desperate that they were committing crimes so that they could be transported — anything to get away from a country which seemed cursed. Besides, the plotters were very badly organised. Every move they made seems to have been known to the police, and was even described in the newspapers.

Thomas Francis Meagher ('of the Sword') who was sentenced to transportation after the 1848 rebellion. From Tasmania, he later escaped to the USA.

The new Treason Felony Act came into force in July, and Meagher was arrested again, along with another leader, Charles Gavan Duffy. Dublin, Cork, Waterford and Drogheda were put under martial law, and a bill suspending Habeas Corpus was rushed through the British Parliament. The Young Irelanders now had to decide whether to drop their plans for a rebellion, or start it prematurely, before it was ready.

When it eventually happened, the rebellion collapsed. There had been no plans, no strategy, and the only responses were from counties Kilkenny, Limerick and Tipperary. On 30 July William Smith O'Brien, with forty armed men, and about a hundred peasants armed with stones, took part in the only real event of the 1848 rebellion, the 'Battle of Ballingarry', in Tipperary. There the rebels found themselves surrounded by police, and were trapped in the garden of Widow McCormack. Smith O'Brien escaped on a stolen police horse, and the remaining rebels fled.

Smith O'Brien later wrote bitterly, '...the people preferred to die of starvation at home, or to flee as voluntary exiles to other lands, rather than to fight for their lives and liberties.' He seems to have had no idea of the effects of starvation, or of how badly the spirit of the people had been broken.

Breakdown of Administration

One effect of the rebellion, of course, was to cause the well of private charity to dry up. If the Irish were so ungrateful as to bite the hand that was trying to feed them, then let them starve. The Poor Law Unions now owed the government about £260,000, and the British Association, which had been paying out £13,000 a week in aid, ran out of funds on 1 July 1848. Gradually the relief system wound down, as the whole weight of assistance fell on the Unions, and the British administrators such as Routh went home. The Society of Friends still gave what help they could, but they were fighting a losing battle.

Trevelyan wrote to the Poor Law Commissioners, insisting that a rate of 5 shillings in the pound had to be struck so that costs could be covered, but Commissioner Twisleton eventually forced him to agree a rate of 3 shillings, complaining that even that could hardly be collected. Trevelyan, however, obviously felt that the Commissioners were trying to get as much money from the state as they could, without using their own resources properly. In September, he told them that Treasury grants to distressed Unions were to come to an end, and there would be no more issues of free clothing.

The wave of emigration now became a torrent, as people gave up hope of remaining alive in Ireland. Trevelyan refused to be alarmed: 'If small farmers go, and then landlords are induced to sell portions of their estates to persons who will invest capital, we shall at last arrive at something like a satisfactory settlement of the country'.

Land was being left waste everywhere, and landowners who despaired of selling simply went, abandoning their estates. No buyers could be found for large estates crumbling under a weight of debt. Trade was at a standstill, and the smaller towns were being abandoned for the cities. An appeal to Lord John Russell said, 'We shall be left a pauper warren...the Queen being the matron of the largest union workhouse ever yet founded.'

Trevelyan, always opposed to Outdoor Relief, had managed to get the numbers receiving it reduced by 200,000. People were brought to workhouses screaming for food, and the buildings were surrounded by crowds of people, who threatened those inside, and seemed ready to riot. Lord Clarendon pleaded for help to Sir George Grey, the Home Secretary, but got the answer: 'It may be that if numerous deaths should occur the Government would be blamed, but there is such an indisposition to spend more money on Ireland, that the Government will assuredly be severely blamed if they advance money to pay debts...'

The government had decided to follow Trevelyan's proposed system of 'operation of natural causes', in other words to do nothing. Lord John Russell wrote: 'We have subscribed, worked, visited, clothed, for the Irish, millions of money, years of debate, etc., etc., etc. The only return is rebellion and calumny. Let us not grant, lend, clothe, etc., any more, and see what that will do...British people think this.'

The Poor Law rules were being strictly applied, including the labour test requiring eight hours' work a day from able-bodied men. Each applicant received one pound of meal a day, and the cost of keeping one person alive for 34 weeks was estimated to be £1. Twisleton, compiling the Poor

Constabulary of Ireland.

What can be more absurd — what can be more wicked, than for men professing attachment to an imperial Constitution to answer claims now put forward for state assistance to the unprecedented necessities of Ireland, by talking of Ireland being a drain upon the *English* treasury? ... If the Union be not a mockery, there exists no such thing as an English treasury. The exchequer is the exchequer of the United Kingdom.

Ireland has been deprived, by the Union with England, of all separate power of action. She cannot do now, as in the days of her parliament she might have done — draw upon her own resources, or pledge her own credit, for objects of national importance. Irish men were told, indeed, that in consenting to a Union which would make them partners with a great and opulent nation, like England, they would have all the advantages that might be expected to be realised. How are these pledges to be fulfilled, if the partnership is only to be one of loss, and never of profit to us? If, bearing our share of all imperial burdens — when calamity falls upon us we are to be told that we then recover our separate existence as a nation, just so far as to disentitle us to the state assistance which any portion of a nation, visited with such a calamity, had the right to expect from the governing power? If Cornwall had been visited with the scenes that have desolated Cork, would similar arguments have been used? Would men have stood up and denied that Cornwall was entitled to have the whole country share the extraordinary loss?

Law Commission annual report, left out this calculation, in case it was said 'we were slowly murdering the peasantry by the scantiness of our relief'.

In December 1848, Clarendon wrote to Trevelyan: '...the statements I have received from (credible) eyewitnesses exceed all I have ever heard of horrible misery, except perhaps that of shipwrecked mariners on a yacht or desert island'.

Rate-in-Aid

1849 was perhaps the worst year of the Great Famine. The rural population had been decimated by fever and starvation. Twenty-two Unions were ruined or bankrupt, and a further forty or fifty were on the brink of collapse. Ballina, County Mayo owed more than £18,000, and had 21,000 people on outdoor relief. In Bantry, County Cork, 2,327 people and 600 children were crammed into two workhouses. People who had paid rates of 13 shillings were now being asked for £13. At this point even *The Times* newspaper, which had always opposed Irish aid, called for 'exceptional relief'. Again Trevelyan offered money to the Quakers to re-establish soup kitchens, and again they refused.

As yet another solution, Trevelyan brought forward a scheme called 'rate-in-aid'. This meant that the more prosperous Unions would have to come to the aid of the distressed ones. The Treasury would also lend £100,000 for further relief. Lord Lansdowne reacted with horror to this 'scheme of confiscation, by which the weak would not be saved, but the strong be involved in general ruin.'

The whole country came together in anger — what was the point of the Act of Union, if Ireland now had to stand completely alone? Why couldn't help be given by English and Scottish Poor Law Unions as well? Twisleton resigned from the Poor Law Commissioners, because the government seemed to be trying to exterminate the population. The Rate-in-Aid Act was passed in May 1849, and the sum to be levied was assessed at a total of £322. 552. 11 shillings.

If blight and famine fell upon the South of France, the whole common revenue of the kingdom would certainly be largely employed in setting the people to labour upon works of public utility; in purchasing and storing for sale, at a cheap rate, such quantities of foreign corn as might be needed, until the season of distress should pass over, and another harvest should come. If Yorkshire and Lancashire had sustained a like calamity in England, there is no doubt such measures as these would have been taken promptly and liberally. And we know that the English Government is not slow to borrow money for great public objects, when it suits British policy so to do. They borrowed twenty million sterling to give away to their slaveholding colonists for a mischievous whim.

* * *

It will be easy to appreciate the feelings which then prevailed in the two islands — in Ireland, a vague and dim sense that we were somehow robbed; in England, a still more vague and blundering idea, that an impudent beggar was demanding their money, with a scowl in his eye and a threat upon his tongue.

* * *

In addition to the proceeds of the new Poor law, Parliament appropriated a further sum of £50,000, to be applied in giving work in some absolutely pauper districts where there was no hope of ever raising rates to repay it. £50,000 was just the sum which was that same year voted out of the English and Irish revenue to improve the buildings of the British Museum.

* * *

In this year (1847) it was that the Irish famine began to be a world's wonder, and men's hearts were moved in the uttermost ends of the earth by the recital of its horrors. The London *Illustrated News* began to be adorned with engravings of tottering windowless hovels in Skibbereen, and elsewhere, with naked wretches dying on a truss of wet straw; and the constant language of English ministers and members of Parliament created the impression abroad that Ireland was in need of *alms*, and nothing but alms; whereas Irishmen them-selves uniformly protested that what they required was a repeal of the Union, so that the English might cease to devour their substance.

THE CAUSES OF EMIGRATION FROM IRELAND.

The Lady's Newspaper, 1849.

Charles James Lever, 'St Patrick's Eve', 1845

To the Irish peasantry, who, more than any other people of Europe,
are accustomed to bestow care and attention on the funeral of their
friends and relatives, the Cholera in its necessity for speedy
interment, was increased in Terrors tenfold. The honours which
they were wont to lavish on the dead — the ceremonial of the
wake — the mingled merriment and sorrow — the profusion
with which they spent the hoarded gains of hard-working labour
— and lastly, the long train to the churchyard, evidencing the
respect entertained for the departed, should all be foregone; for had
not prudence forbid their assembling in numbers, and thus incurring
the chances of contagion, which, whether real or not, they firmly
believed in, the work of death was too widely disseminated to make
such gatherings possible. Each one had someone to lament within
the limits of his own family, and private sorrow left little room for
public sympathy.

Cholera

In December 1848, a man infected with Asiatic cholera had come from Edinburgh to Belfast. He died in hospital there, but cases of cholera began to appear in the workhouse to which he had gone first. Gradually it was carried all over Ireland, and the epidemic reached a peak in May. Advice was given on hospitals and dispensaries, but there was no money to help cholera victims; it was all going to the starving.

Clarendon wrote desperately to Lord John Russell, 'Surely this is a state of things to justify you asking the House of Commons for an advance, for I don't think there is another legislature in Europe that would disregard such suffering as now exists in the west of Ireland, or coldly persist in a policy of extermination.' By the end of the cholera epidemic, 36,000 people had died of the disease.

By June 1849, 768,902 people were on Outdoor Relief, and Irish Unions owed more than £450,000. Discipline had broken down, and clothing distribution had stopped. Queen Victoria contributed £500 to a private fund launched by members of the government, which collected £10,000. But now the Quakers left Ireland, unable to continue. They made it plain that private charity could no longer cope, that the basic essential was for the land system to be completely reformed, and that 'the government alone could raise the funds and carry out the measures necessary in many districts to save the lives of the people'. In all, the Society of Friends had spent £200,000.

CHAPTER 10

1849

Encumbered Estates Act

The plight of the landlords finally made some impression on the government, which realised that something had to be done to allow the system of agriculture to be revived. As long as the estates were crushed by debt, no money would be put into the land, and the value of Irish land had fallen drastically.

The Encumbered Estates Act was passed in July 1849. Under this act, landlords could sell their estates without having to pay off their debts first. A tribunal could order the sale of encumbered land, even if the landlord did not agree, and could grant secure titles to new buyers. It was hoped that the estates would be taken over by English entrepreneurs, who would run them more efficiently, but of 7,489 buyers (up to 1857) only 4 per cent were of this type. Most of them were Irish, from the landed gentry and the professions.

The result of the Encumbered Estates Act, from the point

The rain was extremely unfortunate as it prevented all the fun we selects had promised ourselves in visiting the different places of amusement. The gentlemen indeed braved the weather, leaving the *few* ladies collected in the market house to enjoy the excellent musick of Kavanagh's Band without any chance of dancing to it, for they were wanted to keep order in the hotel, carve for the awkward, serve the drink and so on, and they served too much drink, as long before mid-night there was hardly a sober man and long before daybreak there were hundreds drunken. It was wonderful that no accident happened among them; the gentlemen and a few others kept order. *Our* party was hurt by the Queen, so many had gone in to see her enter Dublin. She was enthusiastically received, showed herself most gracefully and abundantly and was in high good-humour. She has grown very fat, was much sunburned, and too plainly dressed to please the Irish. As she did not come in state there was no procession to signify. The illuminations must have been quite spoiled by the rain. Today she visits all that is worth seeing in the city.

of view of the ordinary peasant, was a new and vicious wave of evictions. The buyers of land expected to find that land empty, so that they could get on with their own plans, usually the expansion of grazing. If they found people still clinging to it, they cleared them ruthlessly. Indeed, the land was often advertised with this deliberate intention. The prospectus for the Martin estate in Galway stated: '... it is believed many changes advantageous to a purchaser have since taken place [since 1847], and that the same tenants by name and in number will not be found on the land.'

Our Welcome
(Elizabeth Varian, published in The Nation)

... We dare not bid thee welcome! hark to that mad appeal —
Our brother's blood for vengeance calls, whilst we ignobly kneel.
'Twere fitting work for rugged hand to strew with flowers thy way
And tattered rags would well befit a nation's holiday!
Hark! to the famine cries, the shrieks of stalwart men struck down,
Crushed in their manhood's noble prime, in all their fair renown;
Thy helpless sister's wailing, the moan of infancy!
Then ask thy conscience, Lady, what welcome waits for thee?

Queen's College, Cork, during Queen Victoria's visit, 3 August 1849.
Lithograph by W. Scraggs from drawing by N.M Cummins

Thomas Brown, of Tullogower, five in family, were living on turnips supplied by his neighbours; his wife could not use the turnips; I found her in a very weak state ....

John O'Brien, of Moyadda, eight in family, lives in a hut built in a bog; the hut is not much larger than a pigsty, the wet pouring in through the walls of it; he is sick in bed, I believe with fever ... he cannot be taken to the workhouse, as a horse and car could not get to his cabin, and men would not venture to take him out in fever ....

William Buckley of Kilcarrol, six in family ... I found old Buckley nearly dead of dysentery; his son had weaving to do, but was not able to do it with the hunger. I gave them the last shilling I had ....

From a report to the Poor Law Commissioners

Royal Visit

Lord Clarendon, Lord Lieutenant of a devastated country, with millions dead and dying and all commercial activity grinding to a halt, decided that a Royal Visit would be good for morale. Whatever about Irish opinions of the government, Queen Victoria herself was quite popular, and the country needed to be given some confidence for the future. Trade was at rock-bottom.

Attitudes to the royal visit were mixed. When people were starving, and the funds of the Dublin Central Relief Committee were completely finished, it seemed a great waste of money to be providing banquets and pageants. On the other hand, perhaps it would raise spirits a bit, and reassure people that they were not forgotten overseas. At any rate, the plans went ahead.

The visit began on 1 August, and went off very well. Crowds of thin and ragged people greeted the Queen (who travelled with her husband, Prince Albert, and some of their children); there was an air of excitement, and they were cheered on their way. A banquet was held at the Vice-Regal Lodge (cleaned up for the occasion), and a huge military spectacle took place in the Phoenix Park. Writing to her uncle, the King of the Belgians, Victoria noted: 'You see more ragged and wretched people here than I ever saw anywhere else.' The royal family visited Cork as well, and were welcomed enthusiastically. The Queen wrote: 'We ... stepped on shore at *Cove*, a small place, to enable them to call it *Queen's Town*: the enthusiasm is immense...'

The climax of the visit was the departure from Kingstown (now Dún Laoghaire, County Dublin) on 10 August 1849. Crowds waved off the royal vessel, and the Queen said that she left Ireland 'with real regret'. The visit had brought some welcome colour and pleasure into Irish lives, however briefly, but of course it had no long-term effect. Clarendon was left with a bill for £2,000.

Famine's aftermath

By 1850, the worst of the Famine was over, and the potato crop was recovering its former strength, although blight still struck at intervals. The Famine affected many future generations, however, and left echoes for years afterwards.

The number of people who died, generally reckoned at one to one-and-a-half million, will never be known. The last census before the Famine, in 1841, had been deficient in many respects, and part of the problem of distributing food in isolated areas lay in the unexpected discovery of large numbers of people who had not been recorded before. The huge numbers of deaths meant that record-keeping almost stopped — no-one could keep up with them, and hundreds died absolutely unknown and unmissed, because their

John Gorman, with eight in family, are despaired of, with hunger and want. They, by much ado, crawled from the workhouse last Friday, barely alive. He acknowledges before God and man that it was the turnip food that gave him and family premature death. They have all the black flux ... I found him with his wife and six children, living in a miserable out-shed, about 9 feet square. The father and three of the children were huddled together on a miserable straw pallet and labouring under acute dysentery.

families had gone before them.

The lowest population loss through death and emigration was in Leinster, the most prosperous province in Ireland, and Ulster came next. Munster and Connacht, the poorer provinces, lost between 23% and 28% of their populations. The counties with the highest death rates were Sligo, Galway and Mayo, followed by Tipperary. One in nine of the population died, and children under 10 and old people over 60, who were one-third of the population, accounted for three-fifths of all deaths.

Some improvements took place in the land system as a result of the Famine. It was more efficient that the smaller farms were to be replaced by larger holdings — the number of holdings of less than 5 acres was halved — but this efficiency had been purchased at great cost. A franchise reform act in 1850 gave the vote to thousands of farmers, mostly those who held 12 acres or more, and they could now act collectively for change. Dairy farming increased greatly in importance, and cattle farmers grew prosperous. However, the landless tenants remained poor and insecure, and still basically dependent on the potato, for another thirty years.

The total costs to the British government of the Famine amounted to £8.1 million, between 1845 and 1850. Less than half of this was grants from the Treasury; the rest was from Treasury loans, which were supposed to be repaid.

Above: Priest blessing emigrants in 1851, the year of greatest emigration when over a quarter of a million people left Ireland.
Below: 'The emigration agents' office — the passage money paid', 1851

However, less than £600,000 had been repaid by 1850, when the debts were consolidated and refinanced. All debts were cancelled completely in 1853, when Ireland was brought into the British income tax net.

However, these huge outlays must be looked at in context. Britain's expenditure on its national defence costs had averaged about £16 million per year since 1815, and its average annual tax revenue was about £53 million. It should also be noted that many contemporary voices, in parliament and elsewhere, argued that the government was not providing anything like enough money for the size of the tragedy. In fact, the greatest assistance to Famine relief came from Ireland itself, through Poor Rate collections, and money contributed by some landlords. At least £1 million was also collected through private charity.

The Famine led to a breakdown of Irish rural society, partly through the greatly increased emigration — about one million emigrated, but again records are very incomplete, and there is no way of judging the full extent. Age-old traditions and folk ways were wiped out, and whole communities disappeared. In 1845, around three million people were Irish-speakers, but this dropped to below two million in 1850. The famine period itself was marked by a dramatic decline in the birth-rate, and far fewer marriages.

The population began to replace itself fairly quickly, once conditions improved, and within a generation many communities had built themselves up again. But the traditional stories of hunger and misery were passed down from one generation to another, fuelling anger against Britain, seen as the author of it all.

This was, in fact, probably the most long-lasting effect of the Great Famine and it acted as a spur to the rebellions and land agitation which broke out at intervals until the end of the century. Another lasting effect, of course, was the Irish diaspora. The large numbers of emigrants provided fertile ground for efforts to win Irish independence, and spread elements of Irish culture far and wide.

Attitudes in Britain, on the other hand, were more mixed. There had been a great outpouring of charity from all over the country, but some commentators were inclined to blame the Irish for being lazy, shiftless, rebellious and ungrateful. Some so-called Christian writers felt that a merciful Providence had acted to clear the land of such worthless rogues, but William Bennett, a Quaker, wrote: 'Is this to be regarded in the light of a Divine dispensation and punishment? Before we can safely arrive at such a conclusion, we must be satisfied that human agency and legislation, individual oppressions, and social relationships have had no hand in it.'

EPILOGUE

The effects of the Great Famine were far-reaching, and include the vast diaspora of emigrants who spread as far as Australia, Canada and the United States, and the pervasive distrust that has influenced relations between Ireland and Britain ever since.

The descriptions of the Famine, and of the deaths and despair which it engendered, are indeed appalling, and can lead to a kind of numbness — it becomes unbearable to read about any further skeletal bodies, overcrowded and noxious workhouse dormitories, desperate and starving hordes, called 'paupers' rather than a more dignified term, overturning soup boilers and trampling over weaker sufferers in the agony of severe hunger.

You find yourself thinking that of course it was terrible, but it could not happen now — we do things better. But it does happen now, and is happening still, and the old arguments are still trotted out about how famine aid is not appropriate, how it doesn't reach the right people, how it demoralises the ability of communities to look after themselves. Technological developments, the ease of modern transport and communications, all the advantages the nineteenth century didn't have, do not seem to have made any difference to the universal human ability to delay, to confuse, to prevaricate, to discriminate, to excuse the inexcusable.

These descriptions are not just part of history. The listless, apathetic groups staring at the ground, the pits filled with dozens of dead, can still be seen in other parts of the world. We have learned less than we should from the Great Irish Famine.

BIBLIOGRAPHY

I was commissioned to write this book as a short history of the Famine, listing the main events in readable form. Of necessity, a lot of detail has had to be left out, and the list of books below is intended to refer interested readers to more detailed historical works.

The most easily accessible primary source is the collection of reprints of nineteenth-century Parliamentary Papers, which was produced by Irish University Press from the late 1960s. Eight volumes of these reprints deal with the Famine period, and they contain Poor Law Guardians' reports, Relief Committees' letters, and all kinds of material relating to the various relief efforts, with many harrowing accounts from all over Ireland. I am grateful to the Gilbert Library, Pearse Street, Dublin, for access to these.

I relied heavily, of course, on material about the Famine published by established historians, and based on solid original research. A basic text is Volume V of *A New History of Ireland* (Dublin, 1989), called *Ireland Under the Union I: 1801 -70*, edited by W.E. Vaughan. This contains eight chapters dealing with the Famine period by James S. Donnelly Jr, and chapters on emigration by David Fitzpatrick and Patrick J. O'Farrell. Equally useful material, relevant to the Famine in Northern Ireland, is to be found in *A History of Ulster* (Blackstaff Press, 1992) by Jonathan Bardon.

The most well-known book on the Famine, of course, is *The Great Hunger, Ireland 1845-1849*, by Cecil Woodham-Smith, originally published in 1962. This is a very detailed account of the Famine, but some of the conclusions have been challenged by later research. Another older book on the subject is *The Great Famine, Studies in Irish History 1845-52*, edited by R.D. Edwards and T.D. Williams, and published by Browne and Nolan in 1956.

More up-to-date research can be found in *The Famine in Ireland* by Mary Daly, published by the Dublin Historical Association in 1986. Cormac Ó Gráda, an economic historian, published *The Great Irish Famine* in 1989 (Gill and Macmillan). Austin Bourke, a meteorologist, devoted years of study to the history of the potato and its importance in the Irish pre-Famine economy, and has published *'The Visitation of God'? The Potato and the Great Irish Famine* (Lilliput Press, 1993). If you are interested in Irish emigration, Graham Davis's book *The Irish in Britain 1815-1914* (Gill and Macmillan, 1991), should be consulted.

Anyone interested in Famine history should try to visit Ireland's first Famine Museum, newly-opened in Strokestown House, Strokestown, Co. Roscommon. The Mahon family of Strokestown House were evicting landlords, and one of them was murdered.

For eye-witness accounts, one book to consult is *The Great Irish Famine*, written by Canon John O'Rourke and originally published in 1874. It was reprinted by Veritas Publications in 1989. Another contemporary account can be found in *Irish Journals of Elizabeth Smith 1840-1850* (Oxford, 1980) edited by David Thomson and M. McGusty.

I would also recommend *A Diary of the Irish Famine*, edited by K.D.M. Snell, (Irish Academic Press, 1994) which reprints a contemporary diary kept by Alexander Somerville.

William Carleton's *The Black Prophet*, cited here, is a powerful nineteenth-century novel published immediately after the Famine. Liam O'Flaherty's *Famine* is the classic novel of the Irish Famine, based on original research by the author.

Other Works Consulted

Benson, A.C. and Viscount Esher (eds.), *The Letters of Queen Victoria (1837-1861),* Vol. II, London, 1908

Boyce, D. George, *Ireland 1828-1923, From Ascendancy to Democracy,* Blackwater Press, 1992

Boyce, D. George, *Nineteenth Century Ireland, The Search for Stability,* Gill and Macmillan, 1990

Deane, Seamus (ed.), *Field Day Anthology of Irish Writing, Vol. 2,* Derry, 1991

Mangan, James J., *Gerald Keegan's Famine Diary: Journey to a New World,* Wolfhound Press, 1992

Mokyr, Joel, *Why Ireland Starved: A Quantitative and Analytical History of the Irish Economy, 1800-1850,* Allen and Unwin, 1985

Mokyr, Joel and Ó Gráda, Cormac, *New Developments in Irish Population History, 1700-1850,* Centre for Economic Research, University College Dublin, Working Paper 17, 1983

Morash, Christopher (ed.), *The Hungry Voice: The Poetry of the Irish Famine,* Irish Academic Press, 1989

Murphy, Ignatius, *The Diocese of Killaloe 1800-1850,* Four Courts Press, 1992

Ó Gráda, Cormac, *'For Irishmen to Forget?' Recent Research on the Great Irish Famine,* Centre for Economic Research, University College Dublin, Working Paper WP88/7, 1988

Robins, Joseph, *The Lost Children, A Study of Charity Children in Ireland 1700-1900,* Institute of Public Administration, 1980

Speed, P.F. *The Potato Famine and the Irish Emigrants,* Longman, 1976

Illustration credits
Colour pages: Quaker tapestry courtesy of the Quaker Tapestry Scheme; William Burke Kerwan paintings courtesy of the National Library of Ireland; 'Another deserted village' and 'The dying drag the dead' courtesy of Sister Anne Therese Dillen OSU; 'Emigrants at Cork' courtesy of the Department of Irish Folklore, University College Dublin; Jeanne Rynhart statue courtesy of Bord Fáilte; 'Queen Victoria leaves Kingstown', 'Nora Dooday' and 'Eliza Morrison' from the National Library of Ireland; folk park ship courtesy of the Ulster American Folk Park; Mission Dolores gravestone courtesy of Seamus Cashman; 'Economic Pressure' by Seán Keating courtesy of the Crawford Municipal Gallery, Cork.
Special thanks to Bord Fáilte and *Ireland of the Welcomes* magazine for assistance in the preparation of illustration.

Sincere thanks to the following for documents and illustrations: Public Records Office of Ireland and the State Paper Office for pages 19, 20, 26, 27, 32, 41, 42, 48, 53, 58, 59, 63, 67, 68, 69, 73, 80, 88, 89, 96, 97, 103
John Gough, Conna for photographs on pages 35, 41
Illustrated London News, pages 6, 22, 32, 38, 53, 58, 63, 69, 88, 96, 100, 101, 102, 106, 110, 131
Irish Journals of Elizabeth Smith 1840-1850 (Oxford, 1980), edited by David Thomson and M. McGusty, pages 11, 55, 64, 72, 75, 126
Bord Fáilte and *Ireland of the Welcomes* magazine, pages 106, 109, 123, 140-141

Overleaf: Continuing emigration — Departure of Irish emigrants at Clifden, County Galway, 1853

INDEX